Dedicated to my mom LaReece, for her love of the English language.

A Day with Diva A

By Theresa Lang

A Day with Diva A exposes readers to the five unique sounds made independently by the letter A. The story helps readers remember to try her five sounds when decoding an unknown word containing the letter A.

Please encourage children to say the 5 sounds "with" Diva A during read-aloud.

Ape	Apple	About	All	Area
(ā ā ā)	(aahh)	(uuhh)	(aaww)	(ae)

Diva A leads a busy, busy diva life filled with glamour and paparazzi, business and fashion, interviews, and, of course, parties.

"Hello, darlings!" she says. "Diva A here. Welcome to my hometown, Letterwood, where I am a STAR!

"Why am I a STAR? Well, darlings, it's because I say FIVE sounds. No other letter in the alphabet does that. Being a diva is THE best—SO much attention. You really should try it. You can learn and practice my five sounds.

"I know! Come. Join me for a day—a day with Diva A."

"I'm up at four in the morning waiting for my limo," shares Diva A. "What's that? You want me to say them? My five sounds? So early in the morning?" Diva A flashes her movie star smile.

"Of course, darling," she replies. "Here we go!"

(ā ā ā)　　(aahh)　　(uuhh)　　(aaww)　　(ae)

Diva A's To-Do List
- Hair and Make-up
- Photo Shoot: magazine cover
- Dance Rehearsal
- Radio Interview
- Book Signing
- Walk of Fame Star
- Fashion Fitting
- Ba-Bling-Bling Consult
- Talk Show Taping
- Gala Awards Ceremony
- After-Party

She waves to the limosine pulling up. "Ah, here's my limo with my manager, Legend I!" Diva A turns to him. "I know I'm attending the Annual Letter Awards tonight, but what else is on today's To-Do list, darling? Check the clipboard, and let's get this show on the road!"

Legend I announces the first stop is hair and make-up for the *Letters Unlimited* magazine cover photo shoot.

"Look at all the shades of pink and purple," Diva A declares. "Difficult to decide which one will be best when I accept the 'Best Letter Award' at the Annual Letter Awards show tonight."

"Only you could be the winner!" says her manager, Legend I. "You are a true diva!"

"Keep my crown straight," Diva A says to her team. She sighs. "I'm so beautiful. Don't you think so, darling?" says Diva A, admiring her reflection. Legend I nods in happy agreement.

"Care to say your five sounds in the mirror?" the make-up artist suggests. "Maybe do each one with a different color lipstick?"

Such a fun idea! "Of course, darling," replies Diva A.

(ā ā ā)   (aahh)   (uuhh)   (aaww)   (ae)

The photo shoot begins. Diva A loves the camera almost as much as the camera loves her.

"How's my make-up? Is my crown straight, darling? My crown better be straight or you're all fired. Ha! I'm joking," she laughs. "But not about my crown."

"Look into the camera and say your five sounds," encourages the photographer.

"Of course, darling," replies Diva A.

(ā ā ā)   (aahh)   (uuhh)   (aaww)   (ae)

Next is Dancing O's dance studio to practice the Diva A Five Sounds Dance Challenge, choreographed by none other than Dancing O herself. The room is filled with students from Diva A's Diva Academy, who can't wait to see their idol.

"Oh, and here's my protégé, darling Sparkling E!" Diva A sweeps Sparkling E into a warm hug.

Sparking E, a little shy, hugs her back while blushing furiously. "Thank you for all you've taught me, Diva A!"

"Alright, everybody. Places! Places!" directs Dancing O to begin rehearsal. "One. Two. Ah one, two, three, four."

"Can't the back-up dancers do all the work?" complains Diva A. "I'm here to look good, not get all sweaty."

"Understood Diva A. One more time for the back-up dancers!" shouts Dancing O. "This routine needs to be perfect for the Annual Letter Awards tonight."

"Whew! That's enough for me, darling," announces Diva A, gulping some water and heading for the exit. On her way out, she continues practicing her Five Sounds Dance moves.

(aahh)
Stick out your tongue and waggle waggle your hips

(ā ā ā)
Move your arms like an ape and spin yourself around

(aaww)
Hands all on your face, so surprised, and stomp your feet.

(uuhh)
Shrug-uh-ugh your shoulders and hop it up and down.

(ae)
Wave your hands in the air cause you just don't care

With glistening sweat on her cheeks from her dance, Diva A begins a radio interview.

"We know about all your projects," the host asks. "The cover of *Letters Unlimited*. A line of regal inspired crowns. *The Real Diva: Behind the Five Sounds* book release. Best Letter Award nomination. Your Top-10 hit single, 'No Sounds Like A's Sounds.' The list goes on and on. But what our listeners really want to hear are your five sounds. Would you? No one says them quite like you, Diva A."

"Of course, darling," replies Diva A. She clears her throat. "I'll do even better. How about a song?"

"Love it!" the host exclaims.

(ā ā ā) (aahh) (uuhh) (aaww) (ae)

No Sounds Like A's Sounds
(To the tune of "Farmer in the Dell")

A says ā. A says ā. A gives us all five sounds and one of them is ā.
A says ah. A says ah. A gives us all five sounds and one of them is ah.
A says uh. A says uh. A gives us all five sounds and one of them is uh.
A says aw. A says aw. A gives us all five sounds and one of them is aw.
A says ae. A says ae. A gives us all five sounds and one of them is ae.

Arriving at the book store, Diva A is ecstatic at the crowd wanting a copy of her book, *The Real Diva: Inside the Five Sounds.*

"Can you believe all these people?" gushes Diva A. "I love signing autographs. See all the pen color choices?"

"Please include your five sounds," begs an adoring fan.

"Of course, darling," replies Diva A, as she softly hums . . .

(ā ā ā)   (aahh)   (uuhh)   (aaww)   (ae)

...and signs the inside cover:

"Remember my sounds!
Love you, Darling,
- Diva A"

Time for Diva A's very own star on the Sidewalk of Stars.

"Finally, some paparazzi," quips Diva A. "Can never get enough."

Diva A delights in the attention, smiles for the cameras, and poses with her star.

"Isn't this just fabulous? See you all tonight when I accept the Best Letter Award at the Annual Letter Awards show."

The screaming crowd chants, "Say your sounds! Say your sounds! Say your sounds!"

"Of course, darling," replies Diva A.

(ā ā ā)   (aahh)   (uuhh)   (aaww)   (ae)

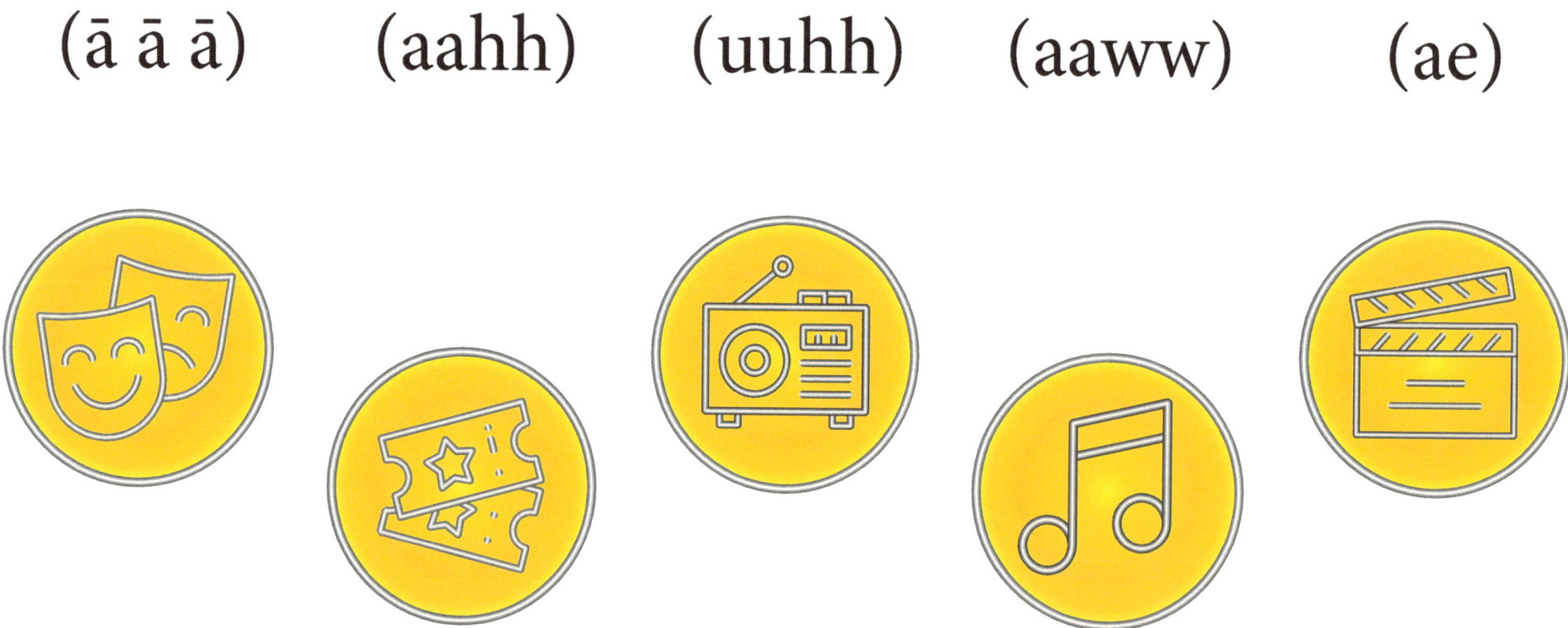

Diva A is not just a star, she's also a business leader. Time for a working company lunch.

"Ba-Bling-Bling Crowns is my pride and joy," she tells her corporate team. "I believe every head deserves a crown. Besides, there's no such thing as too much bling."

"The new Regal Crown Line for your review," offer the designers.

"The quarterly earnings for your review," offer the accountants.

"The retail expansion plans for your review," offer the marketers.

"Excellent job, darlings. Thank you for all your hard work," approves Diva A.

Late in the afternoon, Diva A has a quick wardrobe change before taping the next morning's talk show *Talking Letters*.

"Today's special guest is none other than Diva A," announces the host, Gossipy G. "Please welcome her to the show."

"Thank you! Thank you! Pleasure to be here, darling," says Diva A, enjoying the applause.

"Everyone knows you are one of the busiest letters in the alphabet," continues Gossipy G. "We're excited to hear all about your latest projects and your Best Letter nomination. You seem pretty confident about your upcoming win!"

"I'm the diva's diva," Diva A winks. "Why would I not be?"

"There's no confidence like a diva's confidence!" Gossipy G adds with a laugh. "Now, can we get you to say your five sounds?"

"Of course, darling," replies Diva A.

(ā ā ā)   (aahh)   (uuhh)   (aaww)   (ae)

As evening approaches, Diva A arrives at the Annual Letter Awards show. She dashes down the red carpet into the grand hall just in time to hear the presenter announce, "And the award for Best Letter goes to . . . the envelope please . . ."

"I'm here! I'm here!" Diva A crows as she runs to the stage.

". . . Sparkling E!"

"Thank you, darling! Thank you, darling!" Diva A is still gushing. "I would like to thank my manager, and my parents, and my fans, and . . . and my five sounds!"

But the audience stares at her in shocked silence.

"WAIT! What did you say?!" a shocked Diva A exclaims.

"Uh . . . the award goes to Sparkling E!"

Sparkling E steps onto the stage in disbelief, her eyes brimming with tears for her mentor, Diva A.

In that moment, Diva A realizes that although she has five sounds, although she owns her own business, although she writes her own songs, although she even has her own star, she might possibly not be the best letter. But it's okay. Her protégé, the one she trained since arriving at her Diva Academy, has herself become a diva.

Diva A flashes her movie star smile, hands Sparkling E the trophy, and places a Ba-Bling-Bling crown on her head. Deafening cheers and applause fill the room. It is a standing ovation.

Diva A steps aside. A true diva celebrates the success of others.

What do you do after an awards ceremony? Crash the after-party!
Everybody who's anybody is here.

"Nothing quite like an after party," squeals Diva A. "The stars. The celebrities.
The press. The dancing. It's all a diva could ask for!"

And even though she didn't win Best Letter, everyone still asks,
"Can we hear your five sounds?"
Diva A is in heaven!

"Of course, darling," replies Diva A.

(ā ā ā)   (aahh)   (uuhh)   (aaww)   (ae)

In the late hours of the night, Diva A slips into her waiting limousine to head home.

"Here's to the end of a perfect day, a day with Diva A!" says Legend I.

"I'll toast to that!" agrees Diva A.

Clink! go their glasses.

"Did you enjoy our day together? I do hope you had great fun. I am so glad you joined me for a day, a day with Diva A," smiles Diva A. "Darlings, let's say my five sounds together, one last time!"

(ā ā ā)   (aahh)   (uuhh)   (aaww)   (ae)

Clink!

Dedicated to my dad Bill, for his ability to see everything as alive with a story to tell.

A Day with Sparkling E

By Theresa Lang

A Day with Sparkling E exposes readers to her Diva-in-Training activities, her name sound powers using sparkling dust, and her twin-tastic antics with twin brother, letter I. The story helps readers remember to try all that E does when decoding an unknown word containing the letter E.

Please encourage children to notice E in the practice words and practice the sound being produced during read-aloud.

Note: word lists are not exhaustive.

Sparkling E is a Diva-in-Training at Diva A's Diva Academy. This means Sparkling E is always looking for ways to impress Diva A. Most days, though, Sparkling E spends her time helping all the other vowels say their name sounds.

"Hello, my friends! Sparkling E here. Welcome to Letterwood where I help everyone else SPARKLE every day. How do I do this? Thanks for asking! I'd love to tell you!"

"I know! Come. Join me for a day—a day with Sparkling E."

"So I'm nominated for the Best Letter Award," Sparkling E confides shyly, "but so is my idol and BFF Diva A. She does SO much. I attend her Diva Academy and am doing my best as a Diva-in-Training. So I know she will win.

"But that's okay. I do my best to share like no other letter. Plus, I encourage everyone to be the best they can be. That's enough for me!

"Time to sparkle!"

At Sparkling E's last birthday, she received the best gift ever from Diva A.

"Darling, being one of my best Divas-in-Training, I have a sparkly special gift for you," Diva A tells her with a smile.

Sparkling E opens the box, revealing the word THEY. "WHAT?! For real?!" squeals Sparkling E. "A word of my own to say YOUR sound? I have never been sparklier!"

"Happy Birthday, darling," whispers Diva A.

Before the wrapping paper hits the floor, all the letters join in singing the THEY song* to celebrate.

There is no A in THEY.
There is no A in THEY.
It's an E [whisper] and a Y.
There is no A in THEY.

*To the tune of "The Farmer in the Dell."
Note: whisper "and a Y" when singing because it's a Y-in-Disguise secret!

Sparkling E has one thing no other letter has. As a featured speaker at a Vowel Convention, she tells the others all about it.

"Sparkling Dust! I've got it—all the vowels want it," quips Sparkling E.

"What is it, you ask? It's the finest of powders. It glistens and shimmers, flutters and drifts. It is every color at once, yet invisible like spider webs and angel hair.

"What does it do, you ask? It lets you say your name sound out loud! And it's the best thing ever to share with all my vowel friends," she adds.

"How does it work?!" demand the vowels.

"Simple," explains Sparkling E. "You are alone in a word saying your soft-sound . . . then I appear at the end, sprinkling dust on you and . . . POOF! You say your name sound instead. It's so simple. Try it!

"This is the sparkliest thing ever!" shares Sparkling E, hugging the thrilled vowels.

All the vowels want it. "How much for your dust? Take our money! Sprinkle me! Sprinkle me!"

"It's free! It's free!" she calls in response. "My reward is your fabulous smiles. I have dust for everyone!"

But does she? Nope. Because her bookkeeping skills are the worst. This means she never actually knows how much dust she has. This . . . is . . . a . . . problem.

"I'm so excited to help Dancing O, my idol Diva A, and my twin I," gushes Sparkling E. "Are you ready to sparkle?"

VOWEL CONVENTION

But when Sparkling E reaches into a pouch—it's empty. Nervously she chuckles, "Oh! It must be in a different pouch." She reaches into another pouch. Empty. And another. Pouch after pouch, all empty. "Nooo, I'm sparkle-less!" she cries.

Tears well in Dancing O's eyes and she sniffles, "It is okay. Being friends is more important than saying my name sound."

Diva A nods, "Darling, we understand. When you help so many, you are going to run out once in a while."

"Friendship is the sparkliest," agrees Legend I.

Sparkling E learned her lesson to be prepared and not let down her friends.

Thankfully for Usual U, going unnoticed as usual, he was not included in this fiasco.

"What is this?" asks Sparkling E receiving delivery after delivery—roses and chocolates and notes of affection. "I have a secret admirer?" She blushes. "Who could it be?"

Reader Spoiler Alert
It's X. But there are so many questions . . .

    Will X gather his courage and eXplain his feelings to Sparkling E?
    Will they vacation to eXotic beaches?
    Will they throw eXtravagant parties?
    Will they eXercise to keep their hearts healthy?
    Will they eXcite their fans with eXtreme sports?
    Well? Will they?

If only X will eXamine his feelings. If only X will eXplain them to Sparkling E. Stay tuned readers.

One time, before her twin achieved legendary status, he gave her an incredible gift.

"Ahh Choo!" sneezes Sparkling E. Cough. Wheeze. "No. Not my allergies! Not the night of the Masquerade Ball!" She whimpers and blows her nose. "I have my costume gown, my shoes, my mask, but I can't breathe."

Sadly, Sparkling E climbs in bed and posts online that she can't go.

Seeing the post, Diva A calls twin I. "We have to do something darling! The surprise words we planned featuring Sparkling E are happening at the ball. What if she's not there?" wonders Diva A.

"Not to worry," answers twin I. "I have an idea. Meet me at Sparkling E's and bring more tissues."

When they get to Sparking E's, Diva A sweeps in followed closely by twin I.

"Oh my dear!" her brother exclaims. "We wanted to surprise you at the ball with two words for your soft sound. But since you can't go, I have an idea. The words will still be your soft sound, but we will be the letters. It's the perfect masquerade costume."

"What do you think darling?" asks Diva A. "I'd love to help."

"Ahh Choo!" sneezes Sparkling E. Cough. Wheeze.

"You two say my soft sound? It's sparkling brilliant. Thank you for the surprise! Thank you for helping me!

Ahh Choo! Party on people!"

 **Sparkling E**
Just now

Oh no! I can't go to the Masquerade Ball tonight! I'm going to miss spending the evening with you all!

🙁 589

 Oh no! How awful! We will miss you!

Before Sparkling E discovered her dust and before her twin brother Legend I became a legend, they were kids. Being twins, they played typical twin-tastic antics.

"What words should we do today?" wonders twin E.

"Can I say my name sound?" twin I asks hopefully.

"Not today, little brother," answers twin E. "Today, oldest says their name sound."

"But you're only six minutes older," complains twin I.

"Older is older," quips twin E.

"But I am first in these words, so I think order should decide the sound," continues twin I. "You are being such a big sister. I'm going to tell Dad."

"Order does not matter today little brother. Older is what matters today! We will pick another day for your name sound!" promises twin E. "Besides this is what twin-tastic antics are all about—order does not match sound."

relief	brief
chief	grief

retrieve

believe

achieve

"Hello! I am here for our play date," little Lady C arrives ready for some twin-tastic antics. "So. What is today's order? Who is today's sound?"

"Because you're here, the order is: CEI. Name sound is mine," bosses big sis twin E.

"So not fair," complains twin I. "I am going to tell Mom."

"Today," continues twin E ignoring her brother, "order does matter. We will pick another day for your name sound. I promise."

"Please don't tell on us," pleads little Lady C to twin I. "Remember, changing order but saying E's name sound is the whole point of twin-tastic antics. Stay and play."

Twin E rushes into twin I's room breathlessly announcing, "Today is your day! I have the sparkliest words for this twin-tastic antic! Order for the best of best words is IE. Sound for the best of best words is . . ."

"My name sound?! YES! YES! What's the word? What's the word?" he hollers, jumping on his bed.

"**FRIEND!**" she exclaims. "The first best of best words is: **FRIEND!** What do you think?"

"For real?!" A stunned twin I glares at his sister. "That's not my name sound! It's your soft sound!"

Twin E shrugs like only a big sister can. "This is the ultimate twin-tastic antic. NO ONE, I mean, NO ONE will expect it!"

Twin I is speechless.

"But that's not all," she continues. "I have another best of best words for you."

"I'm listening," answers twin I suspiciously.

"Because you have more of this than any other letter, you are also first in the word: **PATIENCE.** Pretty cool, right?" prompts twin E.

"Well, okay, that's pretty cool," agrees twin I. "I like being first in the best of best words for our ultimate twin-tastic antic ever. Just please remember your promise."

Twin E crosses her heart.

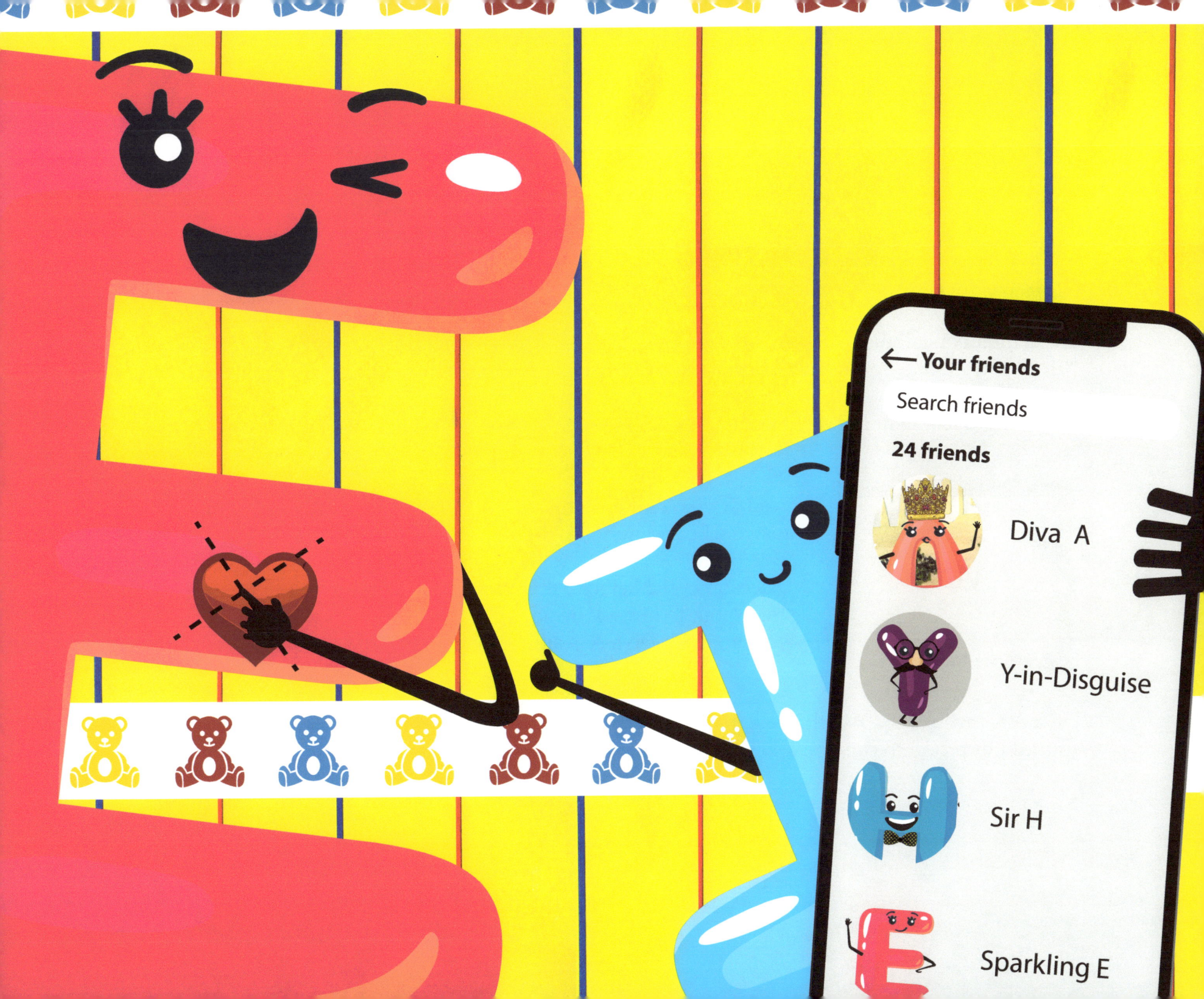

Later, Sparkling E listens closely in a class at the Diva Academy: The Art of Self-Promotion.

"It is an essential skill all Divas-in-Training must master," Diva A explains.

Diva A is always looking for inspiration for new Ba-Bling-Bling crown designs.
"I know—I'll create an accessory line for Diva A's crowns," decides Sparkling E.

She remembers all the times her brother, twin I, let her say her sounds in so many words.
"Time to try make up for that," decides Sparkling E. "Time for twin-tastic antic with a twist."

Sparkling E lets twin I in on her plan. "Count me in," he agrees. "What's the word?"

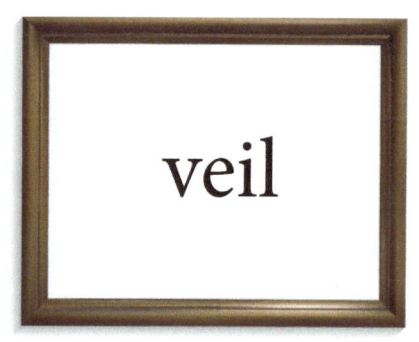

"Veil. My accessories are veils, and we say Diva A's name sound," answers Sparkling E.

"Awesome, sis! Let's do this! And thanks for including me." Twin I smiles, but to himself he adds, "Even though it's still not my sound, working with Diva A is an honor."

Diva A is thrilled. "LOVE the designs, darling! LOVE the twin-tastic antic twist to say my name sound! I'm proud to call you a Diva-in-Training. Keep up the good work, darling."

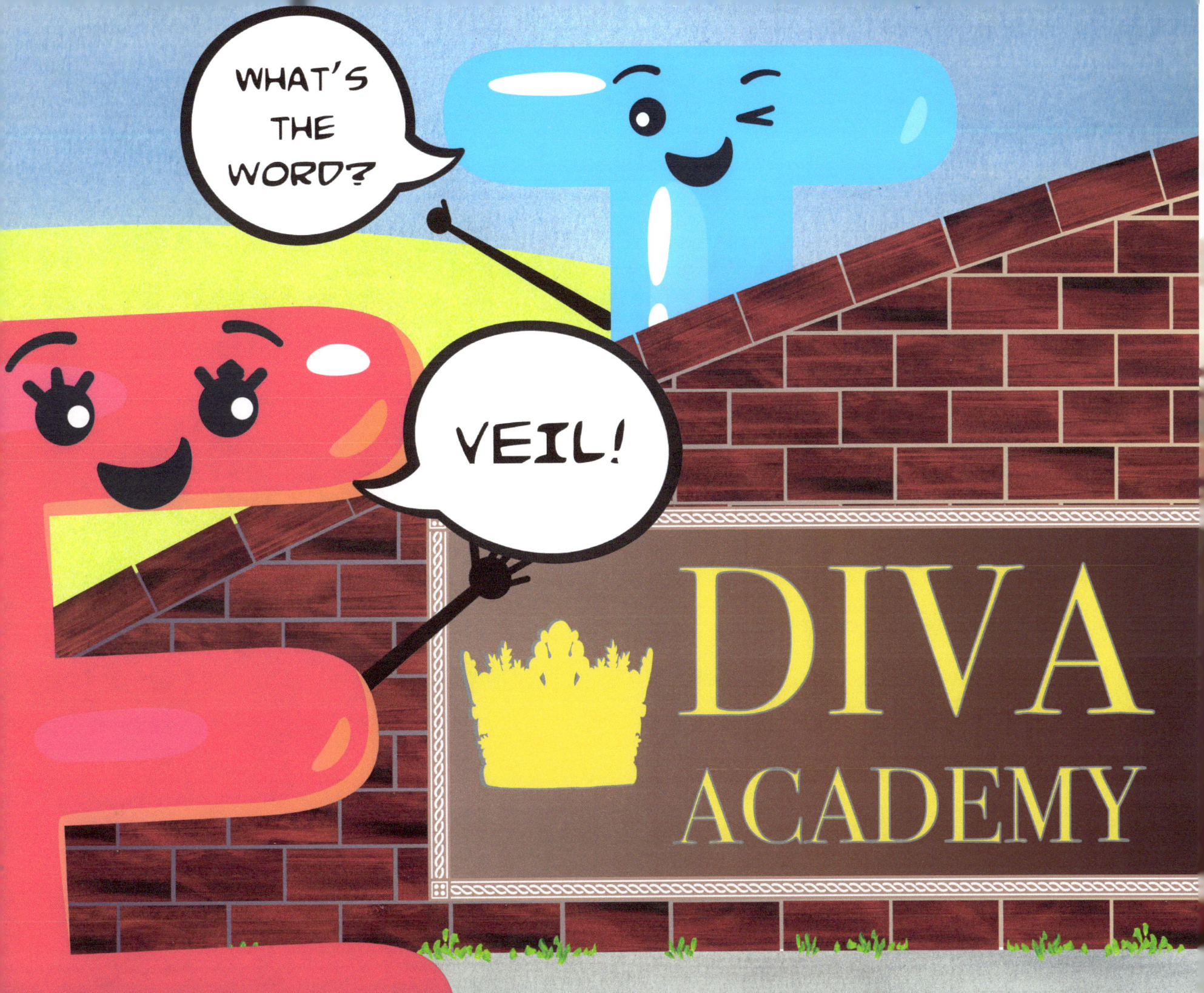

With such support, Sparkling E has the boldest self-promotion idea yet using a twin-tastic antic. But will Diva A approve? Only one way to find out—gotta go for it!

First: Approach Gossipy G and her boyfriend Sir H about joining together for literally the most twin-tastic antic yet. "As long as my TV show, *Talking Letters*, has an exclusive and I get a free veil, it's a deal!" Gossipy G agrees.

Next: Get silent vowel status for GH from Grandpa Z. "I am impressed by your initiative to include other letters in your self-promotion," commends Grandpa Z. "Permission granted."

Last: Present to Diva A for approval. "What a fabulous idea, darling!" gushes Diva A. "MY name sound said by team EIGH? Ingenious. What sparkle you have! Team EIGH saying my name sound is APPROVED!"

(Please note: Sparkling E never did keep her promise to her little brother. Poor twin I. Maybe there will be more in his own story.)

	Talking Letters
	Cartoons
	Info'mercial
	|T...
	Soccer World Ch...
	News of the Worl...
|Documentary|Tal...
	Talking Letters
|Cartoons |Cart...
	Sweets&Mo'
|Rom-Com |Talki...
	Baseball Pre-Season
	News of the World
|Documentary|Talking
	Talking Letters
|Cartoons |Cartoor...
|Info'mercial |Professi...
	|Talking L...
Football Draft Preview
International News
Talking Letters

CERTIFICATE

SILENT VOWEL STATUS

THIS CERTIFICATE IS PROUDLY PRESENTED TO

Gossipy G and Sir H

On this Day, let it be known from henceforth,
Gossipy G and Sir H are hereby
and forever granted the status of a Silent Vowel
with all the associated rights, privileges, and honors.

Grandpa Z

SOUND CHANGE REQUEST FORM

Requested By:

E

Requested Sound:

A

Petitioning Letter(s

E
I
G
H

Request Reason:

...iva-in-Training Course:
...Self-Promotion"
...clude I-G-H with me to say ...
...und

Tonight is THE night—the Annual Letter Awards show. Sparking E and all her friends hold hands and await the for-sure announcement about their favorite diva, Diva A.

The presenter announces, "And the award for "Best Letter" goes to . . . the envelope please . . ."

Sparkling E can see her mentor Diva A already rushing to the stage for congratulations.

". . . Sparkling E!"

What? Sparkling E is shocked! All she ever wanted was to help other letters sparkle.

Diva A herself finally registers that her Diva-in-Training has won the award. The hall is silent, awaiting Diva A's reaction.

Then, Diva A does the most diva thing possible. She flashes her movie star smile, hands Sparkling E the trophy, and places a Ba-Bling-Bling crown on her head. Deafening cheers and applause fill the room. It is a standing ovation.

A stunned Sparkling E looks around the room. "I'm the Best Letter?" she asks in disbelief. But, even she must finally admit, she is the best letter: She shares (all that dust), she plays (all those twin-tastic antics), and she cares (Lady C and team EIGH).

Sparkling E achieves Diva status. This is the sparkliest moment of her life.

What do you do after an awards ceremony?
Crash the after-party!
Everybody from everywhere is here to be seen with everyone!

What is this? Sparkling dust drifts down covering the gleeful letters.
Sparkling E cheers, "Sparkle! Sparkle! EVERY one—EVERY where!"

Dedicated to my son William, for helping inspire these stories while he learned to read.

A Day with Legend I

By Theresa Lang

A Day with Legend I exposes readers to his many roles: Diva A's manager; Sparkling E's twin brother; and capital letter status. The story helps readers remember all the letter I does when decoding an unknown word containing the letter I.

Please encourage children to notice I in the practice words and practice the sound being produced during read-aloud. Remind them (particularly when they are writing) what makes him a true legend: his exclusive permanent capital status.

Note: Word lists are not exhaustive.

His boss? Diva A. His twin sis? Sparkling E. But who is he? Why, he is the best! The one . . . the only . . . Legend I.

"Hello! Hello! Legend I here. Welcome to Letterwood where I am a legend. You want to know the what, the who, the why? Of course, you do!

"I know! Come. Join me for a day—a day with Legend I."

"What exactly makes me a legend? Simple. To find that out, we have to go back to before my legendary status—when I was just starting out.

"It all began when I realized to make something of myself, I had to have something no other letter had," explains Legend I. "But I could never find what that was.

"Until one special day when Grandpa Z came to the rescue. Come with me for the story of the Making of a Legend."

Before Legend I was a legend and Diva A's manager, and before Sparkling E discovered her dust, he and E were kids. Being twins, they played typical twin-tastic antics.

"Can I say my name sound today?" twin I asks hopefully.

"Not today little brother," answers twin E. "Today, oldest says their name sound."

"But you're only six minutes older," complains twin I. "I am first in these words, so I think order should decide the sound. You are being such a big sister. I'm going to tell Dad."

"Order does not matter today little brother. Older is what matters today! We will pick another day for your name sound!" promises twin E. "Besides this is what twin-tastic antics are all about—order does not match sound."

Disappointed, twin I agrees—this time. "Remember your promise," he reminds his sister.

"Hello! I am here for our play date," little Lady C arrives ready for some twin-tastic antics. "So. What is today's order? Who is today's sound?"

"Because you're here, the order is: CEI. Name sound is mine," bosses big sis twin E.

"I thought order didn't matter?" whines twin I.

"Today," continues twin E ignoring her brother, "order does matter."

"So not fair," complains twin I. "I am going to tell Mom."

"We will say your name sound another day," promises twin E.

Disappointed, twin I agrees—again. "Remember your promise," he reminds her.

"Today has to be the day. It has to be," hopes twin I as twin E rushes into his room.

She breathlessly announces, "Today is your day! I have the sparkliest words for our twin-tastic antics! Order is IE. Sound for the best of best words is . . ."

"My name sound?! YES! YES! What's the word? What's the word?" he hollers jumping on his bed.

"**FRIEND!**" she exclaims. "The first best of best words is: **FRIEND!** What do you think?"

"For real?!" A stunned twin I glares at his sister. "But that's not my name sound! It's your soft sound!"

Twin E shrugs like only a big sister can. "This is the ultimate twin-tastic antic." she continues. "NO ONE, I mean, NO ONE will expect it!"

Twin I is speechless. "But you promised," is all he can say.

"But that's not all," says twin E. "I have another best of best words for you."

"I'm listening," answers twin I suspiciously.

"Because you have more of this than any other letter, you are first in the word: **PATIENCE.** "Pretty cool, right?" prompts twin E.

"Actually? Yeah, pretty cool," agrees twin I. He adds, "I like being first in the best of best words for our ultimate twin-tastic antic ever. Just PLEASE remember your promise."

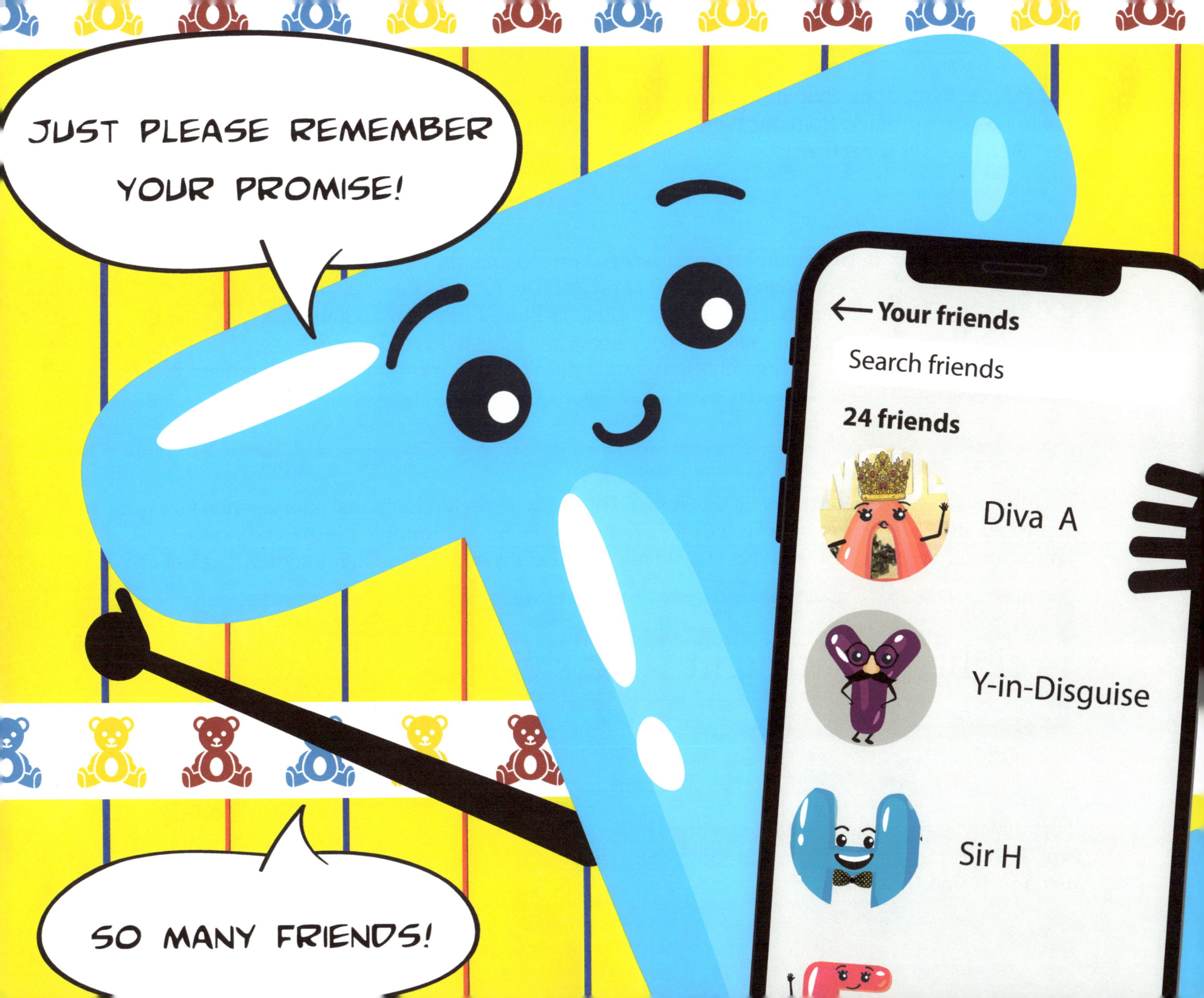

"Wow! Now that my sister Sparkling E is all grown up and going to Diva A's Diva Academy, she is sure to keep her promise from our twin-tastic antics. That's good," notes twin I, as he gets himself together in front of the mirror.

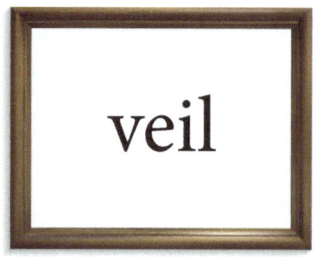

He remembers some special projects he did with Sparking E for Diva A. "Fortunately, in the first project, Diva A loved the veil accessories Sparkling E designed for the Ba-Bling-Bling crowns and loved us saying her name sound. That's good," he adds to his reflection. "Unfortunately, Sparkling E didn't keep her promise. It's still not my name sound in veil. That's bad."

"Fortunately, in the second project, Diva A loved team EIGH saying her name sound when GH were granted silent vowel status from Grandpa Z. That's good," he continues to his own reflection. "Unfortunately, Sparkling E still didn't keep her promise. It's still not my name sound. That's bad."

"Fortunately, these projects meant meeting Diva A. That's good. That's very good," smiles twin I to himself in the mirror. "Unfortunately, maybe Sparkling E has forgotten her promise. I still never say my name sound. That's bad."

But even though she didn't keep her promise, twin I does all he can to support his sparkling twin. One time, he convinces Diva A to surprise Sparkling E at the spring Masquerade Ball with two words just for her soft sound.

But then, he gets a call.

"Did you see Sparkling E's selfie in bed saying she's staying home because of her allergies?" asks Diva A. "We have to do something, darling! She has to be there."

"Not to worry," answers twin I. "I have an idea. Meet me at Sparkling E's and bring more tissues."

When they get to Sparking E's, Diva A sweeps in followed closely by twin I.

"We wanted to surprise you at the Ball with two words for your soft sound. But since you can't go, I have a sparkly idea," begins twin I.

"The words will still be your soft sound, but we will be the letters. It's the perfect masquerade costume."

"What do you think darling?" asks Diva A. "I'd love to be part of this twin-tastic antic."

"Ahh Choo!" sneezes Sparkling E. Cough. Wheeze. "You two say my soft sound? It's sparkling brilliant."

Twin I saves the day. "Party on people!"

After the pollen count drops and Sparkling E can breathe, she asks twin I, "How can I ever thank Diva A (and you!) for masquerading as me at the ball?" She adds, "You're so smart. You must know what she'd appreciate the most."

"In fact, I do know something," answers twin I. "You're never too old for twin-tastic antics, so let's do one for Diva A."

At Diva A's next pool party, twin I announces, "Attention! Attention! As a token of thanks for helping Sparkling E, we present to Diva A this twin-tastic antic word saying her soft sound: **THEIR**."

All the guest ooo and aaahhh approvingly.

"You are too kind, darling," blushes Diva A. "It was my pleasure. You are welcome." Then she waves her arms grandly. "Do you know what? I need that kind of creative thinking all the time. Twin I, would you be my manager?"

Twin I is flabbergasted and stammers, "Yes! Yes I will! Most definitely, I will!"

"Seems to me, as Diva A's new manager, it's time for some of MY name sound words. Especially since as much as she wants to, my sister Sparkling E has yet to keep her promise. No more waiting on twin-tastic antics with her. Time to find another way," twin I shares with Sir H.

"Okay, I have a couple ideas," offers Sir H. "Ask your sister to use her sparkling dust."

Twin I shakes his head. "Hmm. I'd really rather do this without her since she hasn't kept her promise."

"Second option, team up with me and Gossipy G!"

"That's right! GH has silent vowel status granted by Grandpa Z. Let's do it!" hoots twin I.

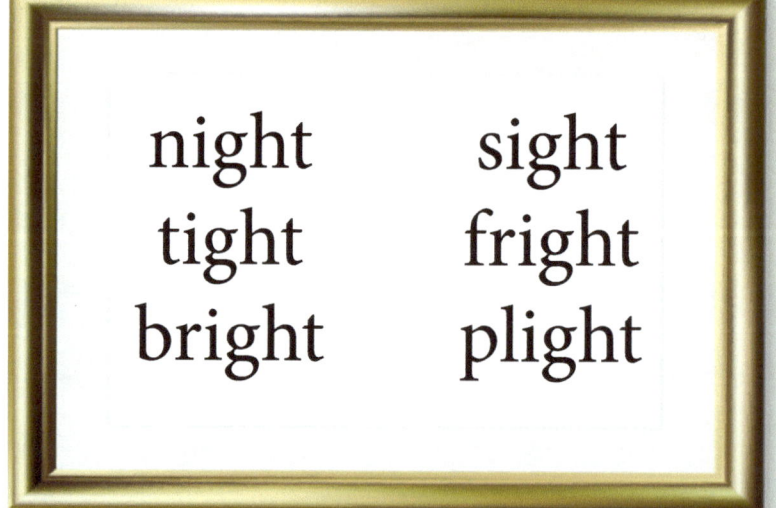

flight   might
fight   delight
right   light

night   sight
tight   fright
bright   plight

Sparkling E is a little stunned, a little hurt, but not surprised when twin I tells her about working with Gossipy G and Sir H. "You're right. I haven't kept my promise. I'm sorry," she apologizes. "I'd really like to have a twin-tastic antic word with your name sound. What say you?"

"I can't stay mad at my big sis," smiles twin I.
"Please join us for a word."

"I have the best little brother in all of Letterwood,"
sparkles Sparkling E.

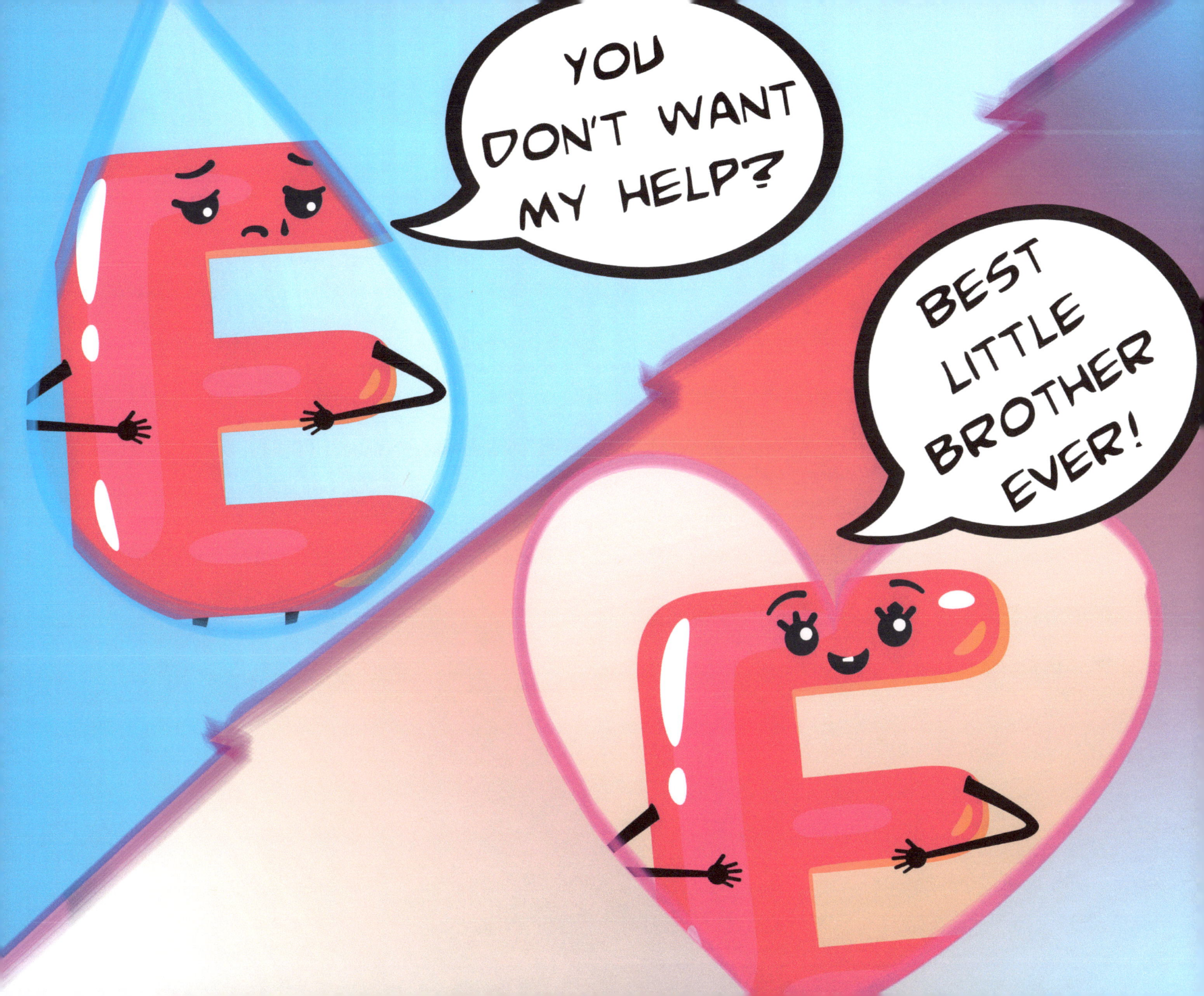

But twin I wonders and wonders when he will ever get to say his own name sound, all by himself. He frets and worries for days.

Finally, the very best, most amazing grandfather in all of Letterwood, Grandpa Z, notices his sads.

"What is it, twin I? How can I help?"

"I am the only letter in the entire alphabet that never says their own name sound," twin I explains with a frown. "It's never just me, by myself. Why?

Grandpa Z laughs. "Haven't you ever noticed? Everyone says your name sound all the time!"

"They do?" twin I says, surprised.

"I say it whenever I say anything about myself!" Grandpa Z continues. "See? I just said it three times!"

Twin I gasps. "When you said, 'I say it,' you're saying my name sound!"

"Yes! Everyone does! It's the word, all by itself, that we use for ourselves! And, to top it off, it's always capital!"

Twin I laughs out loud. "What word do we use for ourselves? I! We use 'I' for ourselves! This is great!"

He jumps up and grabs his pompoms, spreads his arms out to his sides, and points his feet with heels together and toes out. He IS the capital letter **I**! He yells his cheer:

"**I**! It's a capital every time. **I**! It's a capital all alone."

"**I**! It's a capital every time. **I**! It's a capital all alone."

"All together now!"

"**I**! It's a capital every time. **I**! It's a capital all alone."

"**I**! It's a capital every time. **I**! It's a capital all alone."

Grandpa Z gives twin I a big high-five and says, "From time immemorial, you have always been what we all need. It's legendary, in fact. From henceforth you shall be known as: Legend I. Congratulations!"

EXCLUSIVE

PERMANENT

CAPITAL

Tonight is THE night—the Annual Letter Awards show.

Legend I is rooting for his twin sis Sparkling E to win, but knows his boss Diva A expects to win. Who will it be?

The presenter announces, "And the award for "Best Letter" goes to . . . the envelope please . . . Sparkling E!"

Like everyone else, Legend I is shocked. He scrambles to stop Diva A, but even he can't keep her from making the HUGE mistake of thinking she won. But then he cheers as Diva A shows her true diva colors by embracing and congratulating Sparkling E, even placing a Ba-Bling Bling crown on her head.

Deafening cheers and applause fill the room. It is a standing ovation. No one cheers louder or is prouder than Legend I. He cheers for his sister—remembering all their twin-tastic antics and all she does for others. He cheers for his boss—seeing her accept losing with diva-style grace. He knows he will continue being a legend for them both.

What do you do after an awards ceremony?
Crash the after-party!
Everybody from everywhere is here to be seen with everyone!

"May I have this dance?" a proud Legend I asks his twin sister Sparkling E.

"You know you can," winks Sparkling E. "But remember, even though you are a legend, you will always be my little brother." She continues, "We should do more twin-tastic antics."

Legend I rolls his eyes and laughs. "Only if we say my name sound."

"*I* will if you will!" giggles Sparkling E.

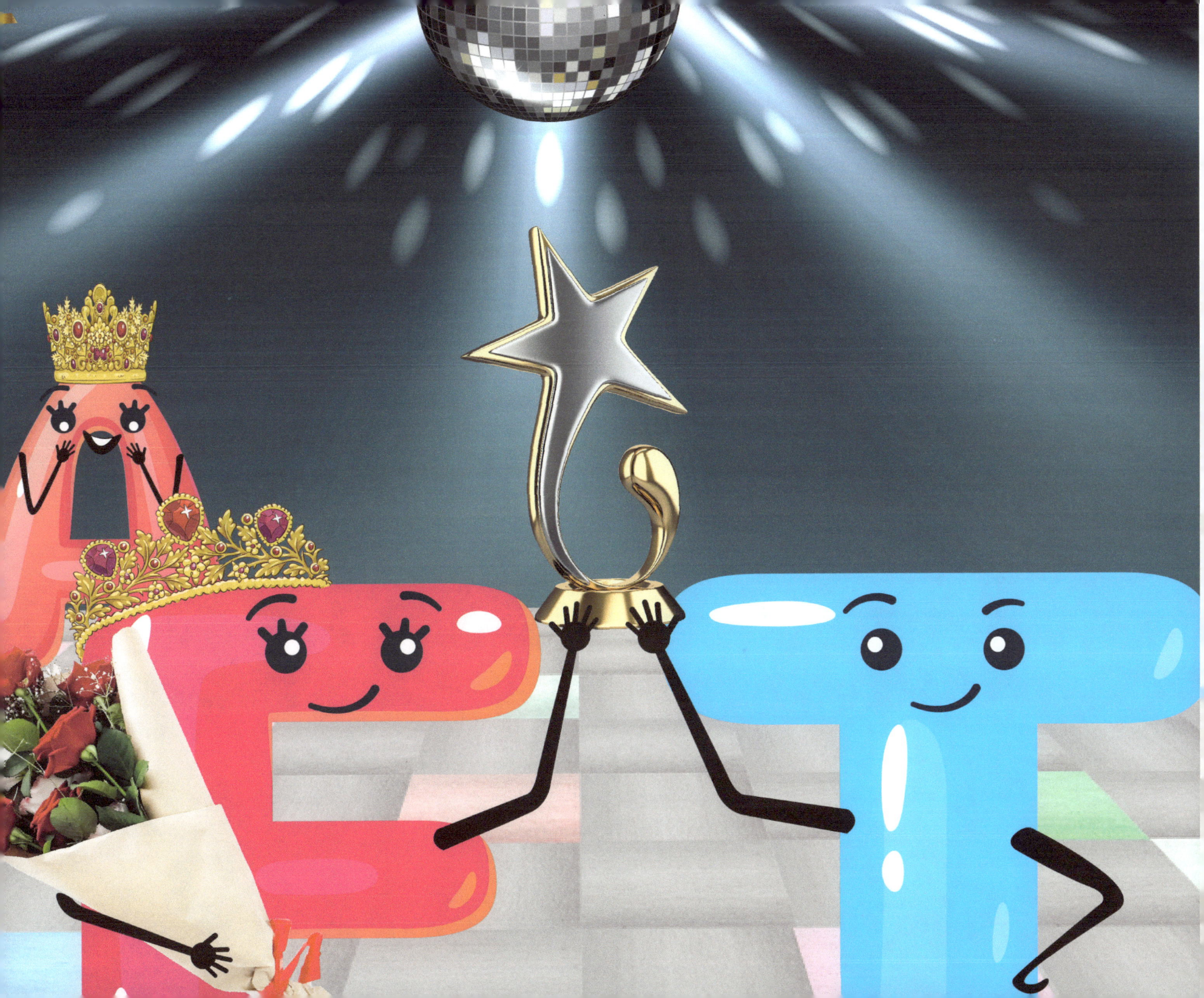

Let's Play: NAME THAT SOUND

See a word. Guess what sound the twins E and I are saying.

Ready? Set! Go!

What sound are Twins E and I saying?

weigh   friend   chief   receipt

Extra challenge:

their   either   neither

*Find more words on the twin-tastic antic pages.

Dedicated to my son Richard, for his desire to read more to learn more.

A Day with Dancing O

By Theresa Lang

A Day with Dancing O exposes readers to O's inclusion with other vowels resulting in an array of different sounds—some predictable, some not. The story introduces the concept of two vowels producing one sound, plus OU/OW/OO. It helps readers remember to try all O does when decoding an unknown word containing the letter O.

Please encourage children to notice the sounds O makes with other vowels in the practice words, plus how her "dances" impact two vowels together during read-aloud.

Note: Word lists are not exhaustive.

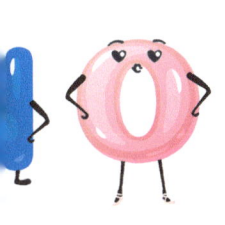

Need to brush up on a waltz for an upcoming wedding? Need a new routine for a hip-hop video? Need a dance challenge for social media? Time for lessons from Dancing O.

"Hello dance-lettes! Dancing O here. Welcome to Letterwood, where I make stars dance. No, not stars in the sky stars—Letterwood stars. I work with all the vowels, A-E-I-O-U, and Y, and even W. So? Ready to hit the dance floor?

"I know! Come. Join me for a day—a day with Dancing O."

"A dancer's shoes are critical for success," begins Dancing O. "When I started dancing, it was impossible to find shoes to fit my teeny-tiny, itty-bitty feet. But did that stop me? No! I opened my own shoe shop, Twinkle Toes." She winks. "Only the most exquisite designs with the highest quality materials are sold in all sizes, even the tiniest."

"Best of all? Everyone gets 50% off a pair with their first dance lesson package purchase," boasts Dancing O.

Dancing O is the undefeated champion of the hit TV dance competition show *1-2-3, Dance!*

"This year I take on the ultimate challenge," boasts Dancing O. "I am choosing a partner who cannot dance, and I will still win. Err, WE will win. I know just the letter. Here he comes now with those gigantic, enormous, BIG feet, making him the perfect choice."

"Would you like to be my dance—" she begins.

Before she finishes, Usual U interrupts. "I would like nothing more than to dance with you!"

He whispers to himself, "Anything for my secret crush."

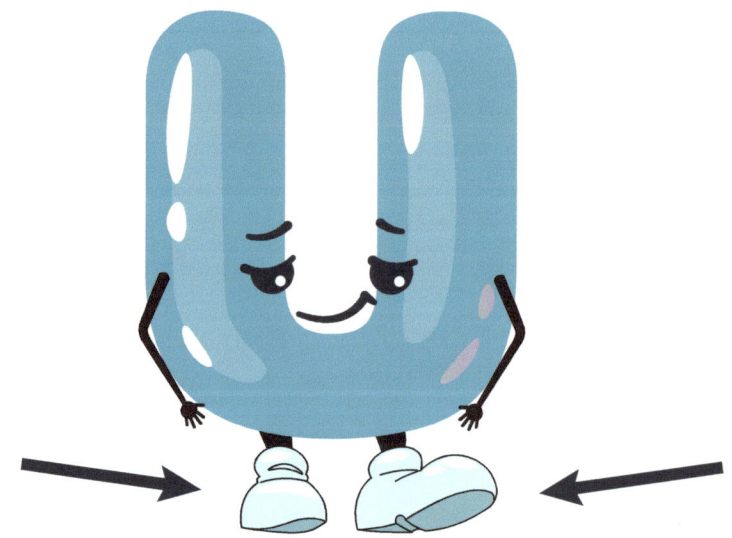

With each practice, Usual U tries and tries. With each practice, Dancing O tries and tries. But with each practice, sadly, it is obvious, his feet are too big. He cannot help stepping on her teeny-tiny, itty-bitty feet.

With tears in her eyes, she cries, "OUch!" With tears in his eyes, he cries, "I am so sorry." Even so, they keep trying.

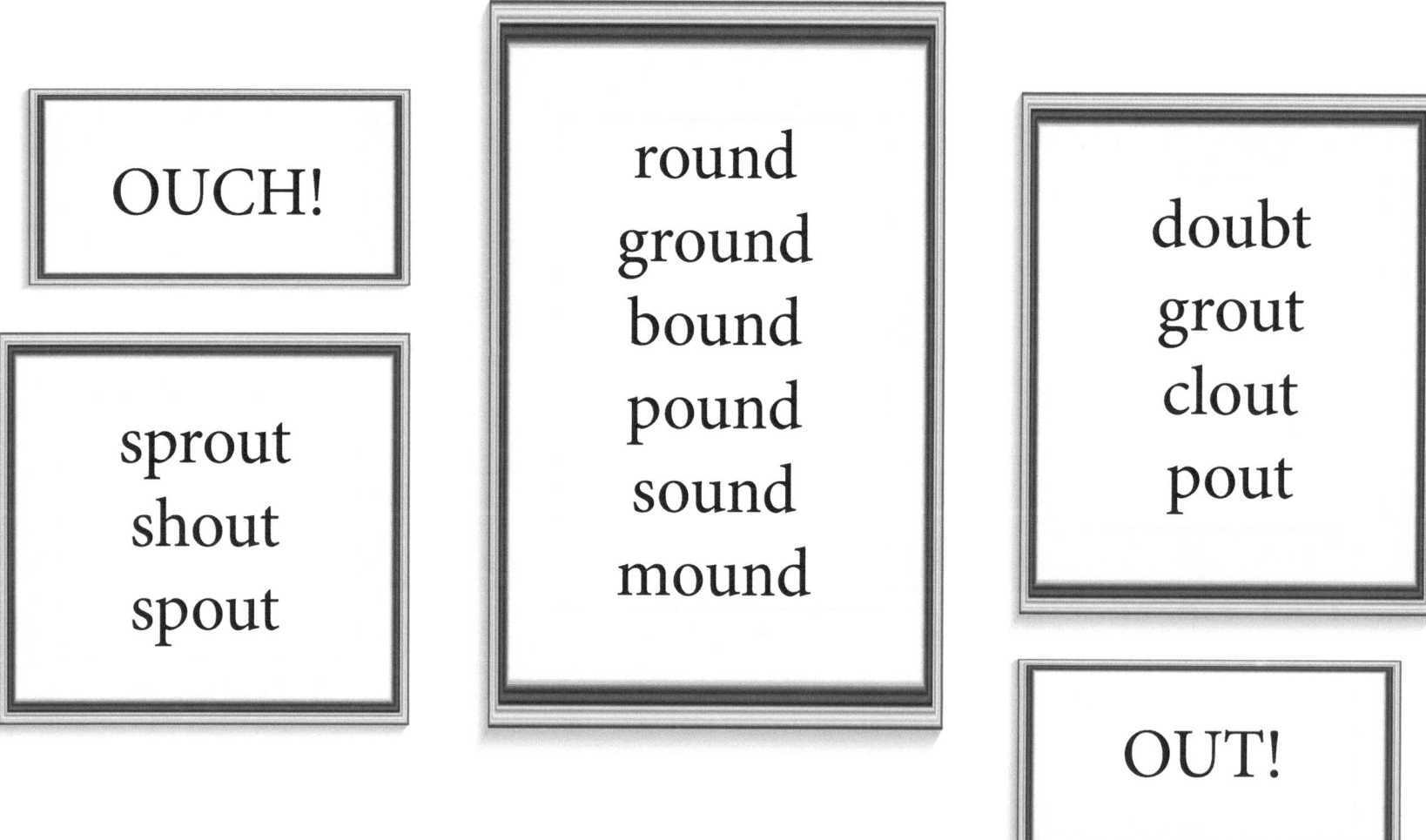

OUCH!

sprout
shout
spout

round
ground
bound
pound
sound
mound

doubt
grout
clout
pout

OUT!

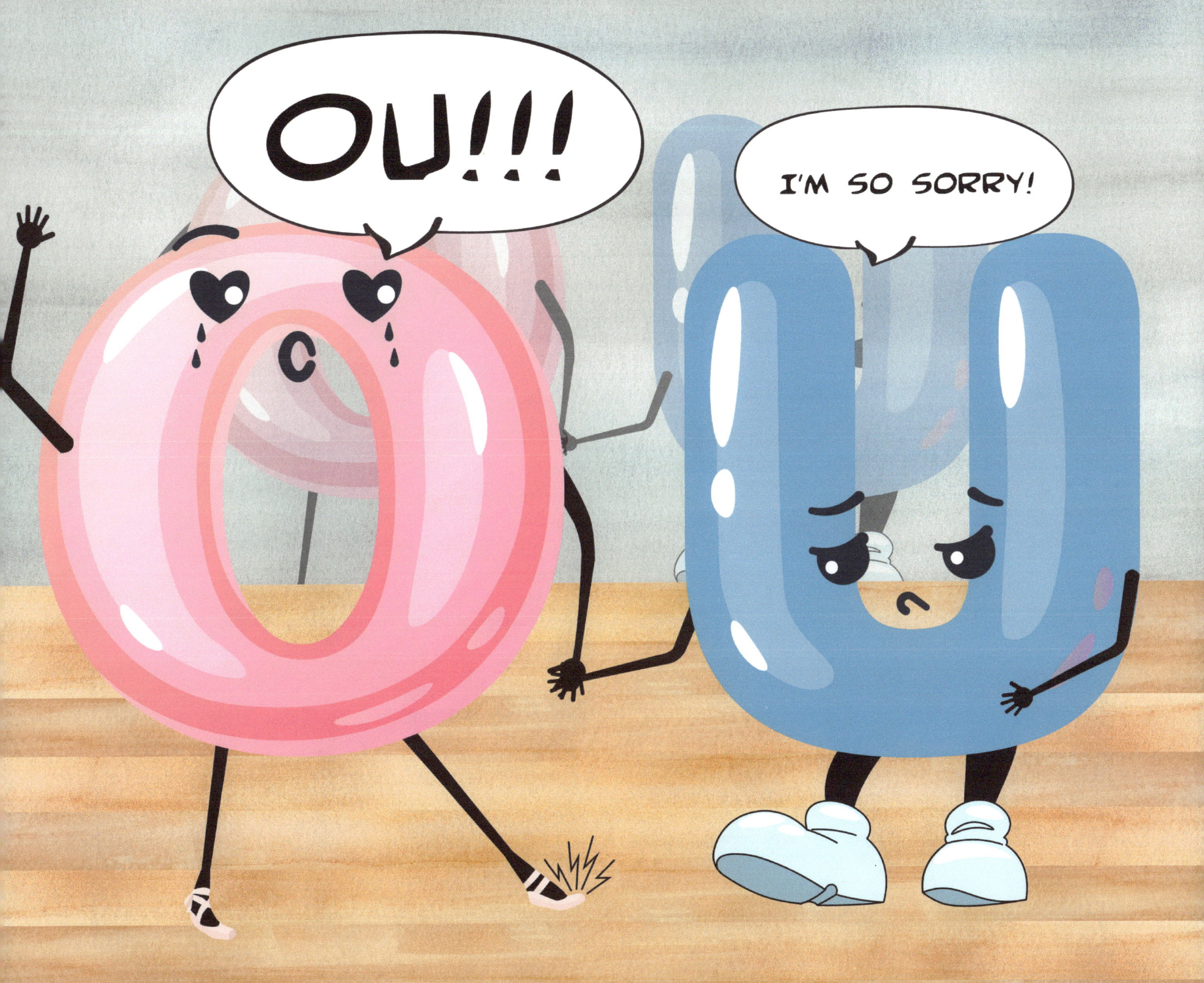

After weeks of preparation, Dancing O must admit teaching Usual U to dance is hopeless.

"Winning the competition with Usual U is impossible," she cries. Her crushed toes, twisted ankles, and bruised teeny-tiny, itty-bitty feet can take no more.

She tries to let Usual U down gently. "You have practiced so much, but we both know this will not work."

With a broken heart, he admits she is right. He will never be Dancing O's partner. As he leaves with a heavy sigh and tears running down his cheeks, he pines, "I hope I find true love someday."

ounce
bounce
pounce
trounce

mount
count

loud
cloud

Dancing O feels sad, so she promises herself to help Usual U someday. But right now, she has a competition to win.

"What am I going to do? Where is a replacement? Who can I find?" she asks feverishly. "Ah Ha! What? Where? Who? I know . . . Ms. W!"

Ms. W agrees to step in the dance and not step on those teeny-tiny, itty-bitty feet. They are unstoppable: the timing, the footwork, the grace.

The judges' decision? First Place and Grand Prize go to, drum roll please, Dancing O and Ms. W! "Thank you! Thank you! I knew I could—Err, WE could do it," beams Dancing O. Ms. W rolls her eyes.

But letters listening closely during their dance hear Dancing O still saying, "OW!" Her feet still aching from dancing with Usual U.

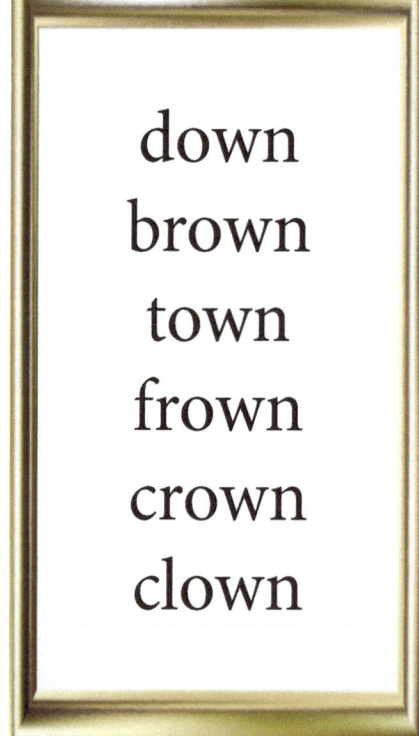

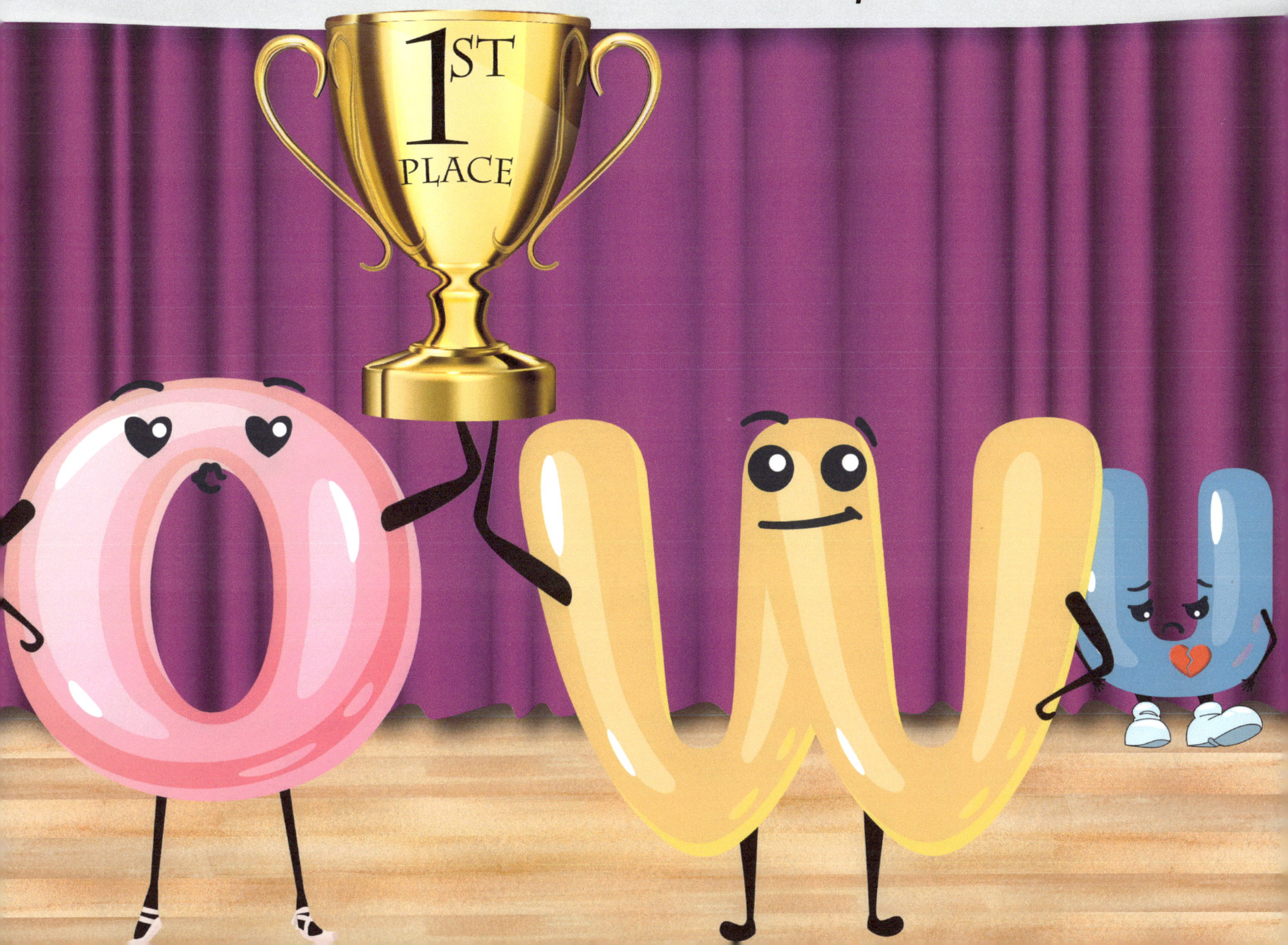

Oh goodness! There is a problem in Letterwood, and it is tearing friendships apart. When vowels are walking to their dance lessons, they keep talking at the same time—neither one waiting for the other, neither one listening to the other. How rude!

"Who should talk?" they complain to Dancing O.

She is surprised they do not know. She responds, "Be polite. Take turns. While you both walk, the first vowel talks and the second vowel listens. I call it the Walk-n-Talk Dance."

"Excellent solution," everyone agrees. "Yay! Our friendships are saved."

ail/sail   eat/heat   oat/coat

The Walk-n-Talk Dance is a huge success. But changing dance moves happens all the time.

Dancing together one day, Sparkling E asks Diva A, "Remember the birthday gift you gave me? The sparkliest gift ever! The word THEY spelled T-H-E-Y—where I say YOUR name sound."

"Of course I remember, darling," answers Diva A.

"I want to thank you for your generous gift," continues Sparkling E. "I propose a slightly changed Walk-n-Talk Dance step."

They show it to Dancing O for approval. She says it looks (and sounds) fantastic! Flashing her movie star smile, Diva A agrees. Sparkling E walks first while Diva A talks. It is a **GREAT** big hit!

great
break
steak

After a few dances, Diva A has another dance change idea for Sparkling E.

"What if you still walk first AND you talk first, BUT you say your soft sound?" Her eyes are bright with excitement. She adds, "It's our own version of a twin-tastic antic."

"Sounds lovely!" agrees Sparkling E. "Let's show it to Dancing O!"

Dancing O gives her wholehearted approval.

Sparkling E and Diva A are delighted. "This is the best dance ever. This is the most fun ever. We are BFF's forever!" they giggle together.

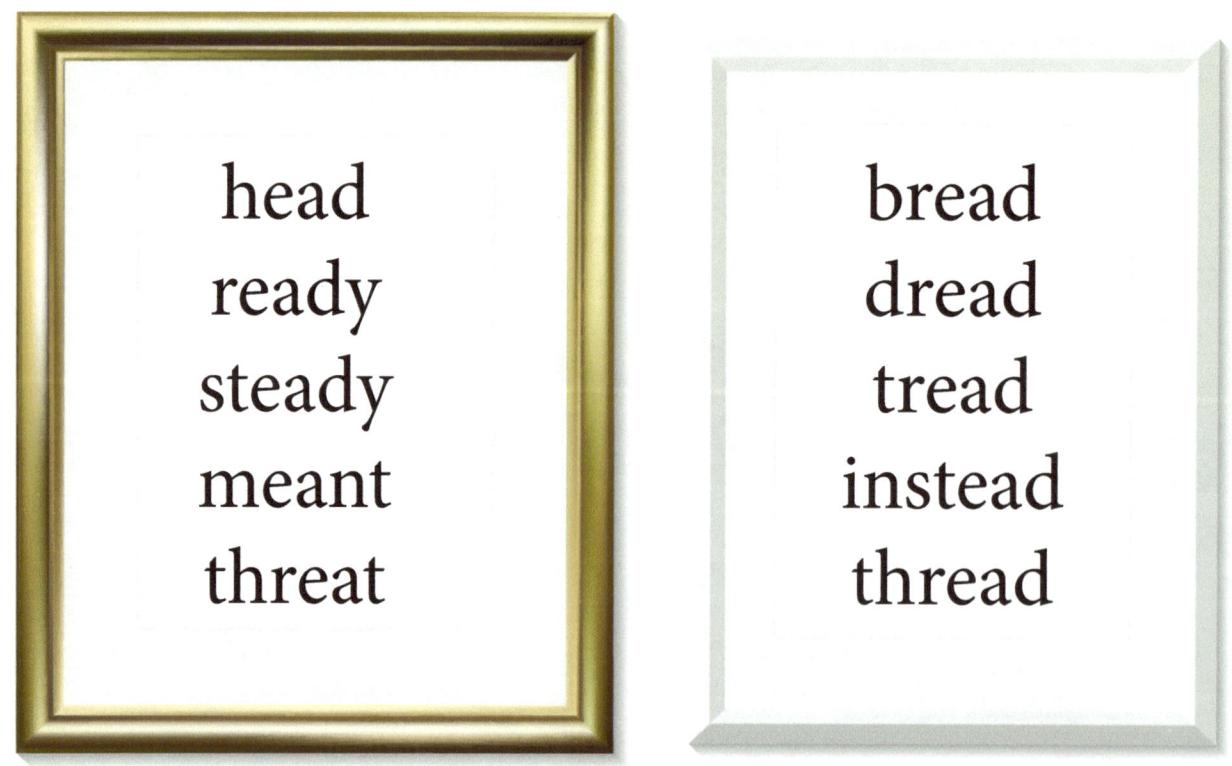

head	bread
ready	dread
steady	tread
meant	instead
threat	thread

"I suppose it had to happen," remarks Dancing O after Sparkling E and Diva A change the Walk-n-Talk Dance rules. "Wonder what else my dancers will come up with?"

She is right. Vowels change up which one talks and have fun doing it. "We are just being extra polite," they explain.

"Well, in that case, I approve. Polite is always best," she cheers.

Eventually she likes the new dance steps so much, she wants to try it herself, and she knows just the letter to ask. "Time to make good on my promise to Usual U," she shares with Sparkling E and Diva A.

Usual U can hardly believe Dancing O wants to dance with him again. She assures him, "I'll walk while you talk. Just a few words so my teeny-tiny, itty-bitty feet survive."

Usual U cannot stop smiling. "How wonderful is this?" he thinks. "Even though we can't be partners, we can still be friends."

coupe   soup   troupe

"Dancing is my passion!" squeals Dancing O. "In some dances I am so good and so fast, I don't need another vowel partner!"

She really can dance fast. She can dance so fast she looks like two dancers. But she rarely says her sounds when she dances like this.

"I was able to dance with Usual U for so few words," she announces, "that I will dedicate my solo speed dancing to him and say his sounds."

Usual U blushes whenever he hears one of his three sounds made by speed Dancing O.

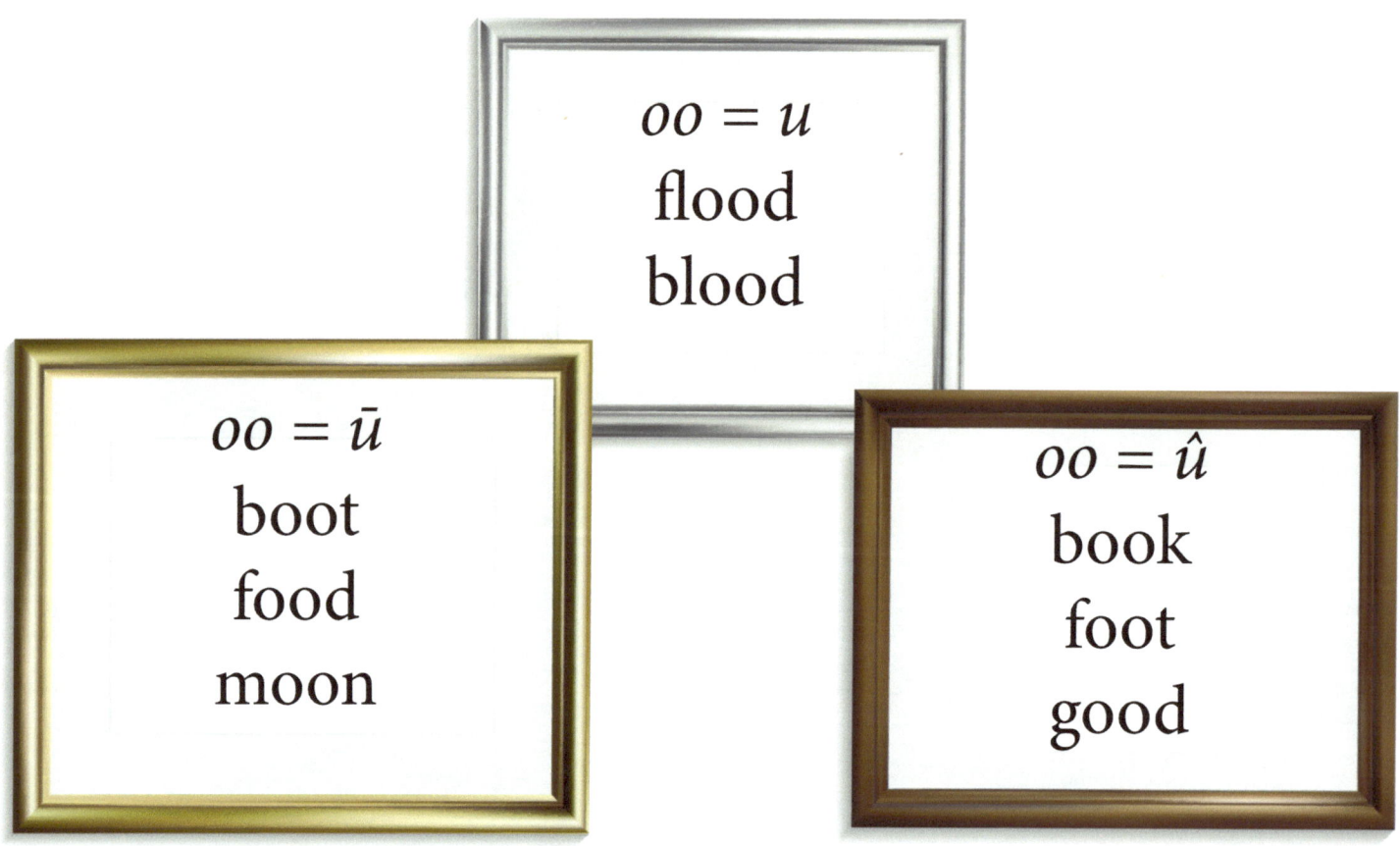

$oo = u$

flood

blood

$oo = \bar{u}$

boot

food

moon

$oo = \hat{u}$

book

foot

good

Tonight is THE night—the Annual Letter Awards show. Before the Best Letter winner announcement is the dance portion of the program.

"Shh, everyone! It is time for Diva A's dance challenge," breathes Dancing O backstage. "This is going to be epic!!"

The Dance-lettes enter center stage. "Lights! Curtains! Music! DANCE!" she directs.

The audience watches in awe at the flawless steps. They cannot resist the music and the moves. They stand—they clap—they groove! Cheers erupt as the challenge ends. It. Is. EPIC!

Dancing O steps into the spotlight, bows grandly, blows kisses and shouts, "Remember, 50% off all Twinkle Toe shoes with your first dance lesson package purchase!"

What do you do after an awards ceremony?
Crash the after-party!
Everybody from everywhere is here to be seen with everyone!

Even though Diva A didn't win Best Letter,
her dance challenge choreographed by Dancing O is tonight's favorite dance.

"Look at all these dancing stars!" cries Dancing O. Delighted, she dances the night away.

Dedicated to my grandma Olive, for her love of reading
stories aloud to me, no matter how old I was.

A Day with Usual U

By *Theresa Lang*

A Day with Usual U exposes readers to the sounds U makes with Dancing O and Queen Q and to his own word YOU. The story helps readers remember to try all that U does when decoding an unknown word containing the letter U.

Please encourage children to notice U in the practice words and practice the sound being produced during read-aloud.

Note: Word lists are not exhaustive.

Ah, poor Usual U—a quiet and sincere fellow who prefers working behind the scenes. He has always been self-conscious about his big, very big, feet, making him terribly unconfident and shy.

"Um. Hi there. Usual U here. Welcome to Letterwood where I prefer to go unnoticed.

"Not everyone can be a star, or a legend, or sparkle, or dance. Not everyone wants the spotlight. This means I go about my work without attention. This means I go about my day unnoticed. This doesn't mean I'm not important. It just means I'm usual. And I like it that way.

"I know. Come. Join me going unnoticed for a day—a day with Usual U."

"I am so sorry. I must apologize for my large feet. I must warn you to watch your toes," begins Usual U to everyone he meets. "Seems I'm either stepping on other's feet or tripping on my own." Ah. Poor Usual U.

Sadly, Usual U's baby sister Lovey V teases him, "Your feet are maaaaaass-ive. Your feet are enormous. Your feet are clod-hoppers." This does nothing for Usual U's self-esteem.

But thankfully, Usual U's big sis Ms. W is around. "Don't listen to her. She's just jealous of all you do without fanfare or attention. No reason to apologize. Just be you."

He smiles. "Time for a walk to Dancing O's dance studio" decides an encouraged Usual U. "Maybe I will see her," he hopes as he stumble-tumbles down the sidewalk.

Usual U has such a crush on Dancing O. As much as he tries to be unnoticed, everyone notices when he's around her. He smiles and he blushes. It is adorable.

"I wonder if Dancing O has picked her dance partner for this year's TV dance competition show *1-2-3 Dance!*?" thinks Usual U. "She says this year will be her ultimate challenge."

As he approaches her dance studio, she calls out, "Would you like to be my dance—"

But before she finishes, Usual U blurts out, "I would like nothing more than to dance with you!" He whispers to himself, "Anything for my secret crush."

With each practice, Usual U tries and tries. With each practice, Dancing O tries and tries. Sadly, it is obvious his feet are too big. He cannot stop stepping on her teeny-tiny, itty-bitty, dainty feet.

With tears in her eyes, she cries, "OUch!" With tears in his eyes, he cries, "I am so sorry." Even so, they keep trying.

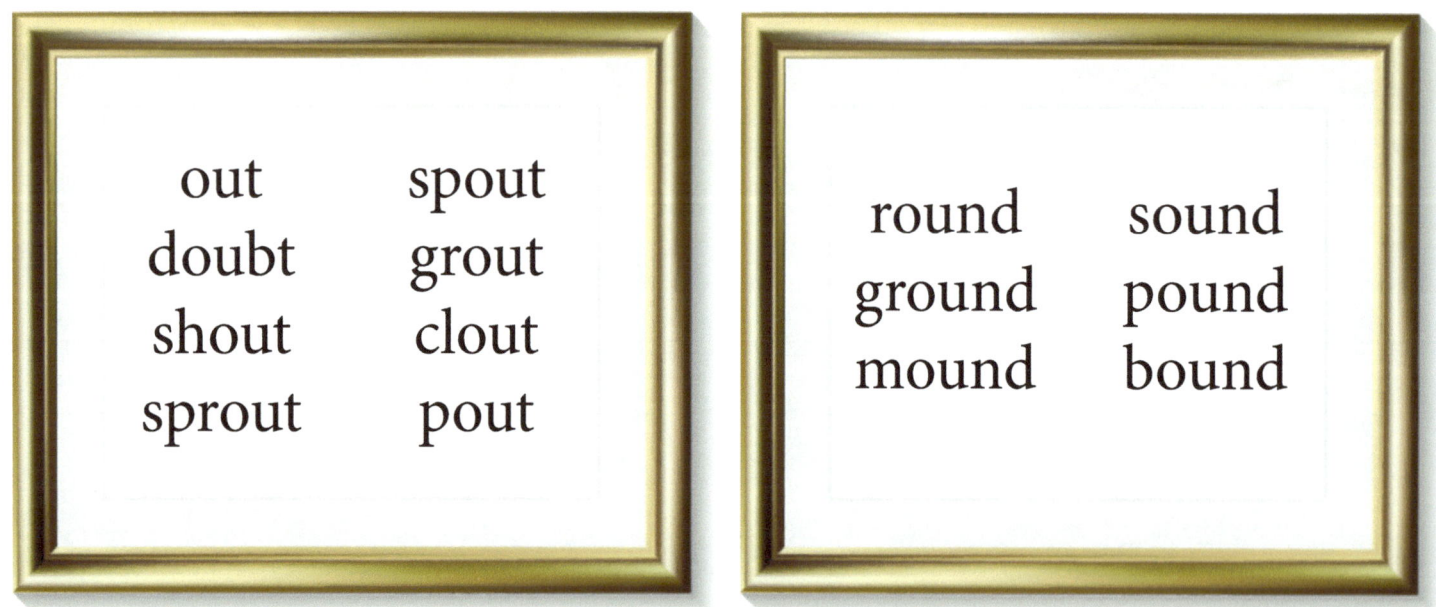

out	spout
doubt	grout
shout	clout
sprout	pout

round	sound
ground	pound
mound	bound

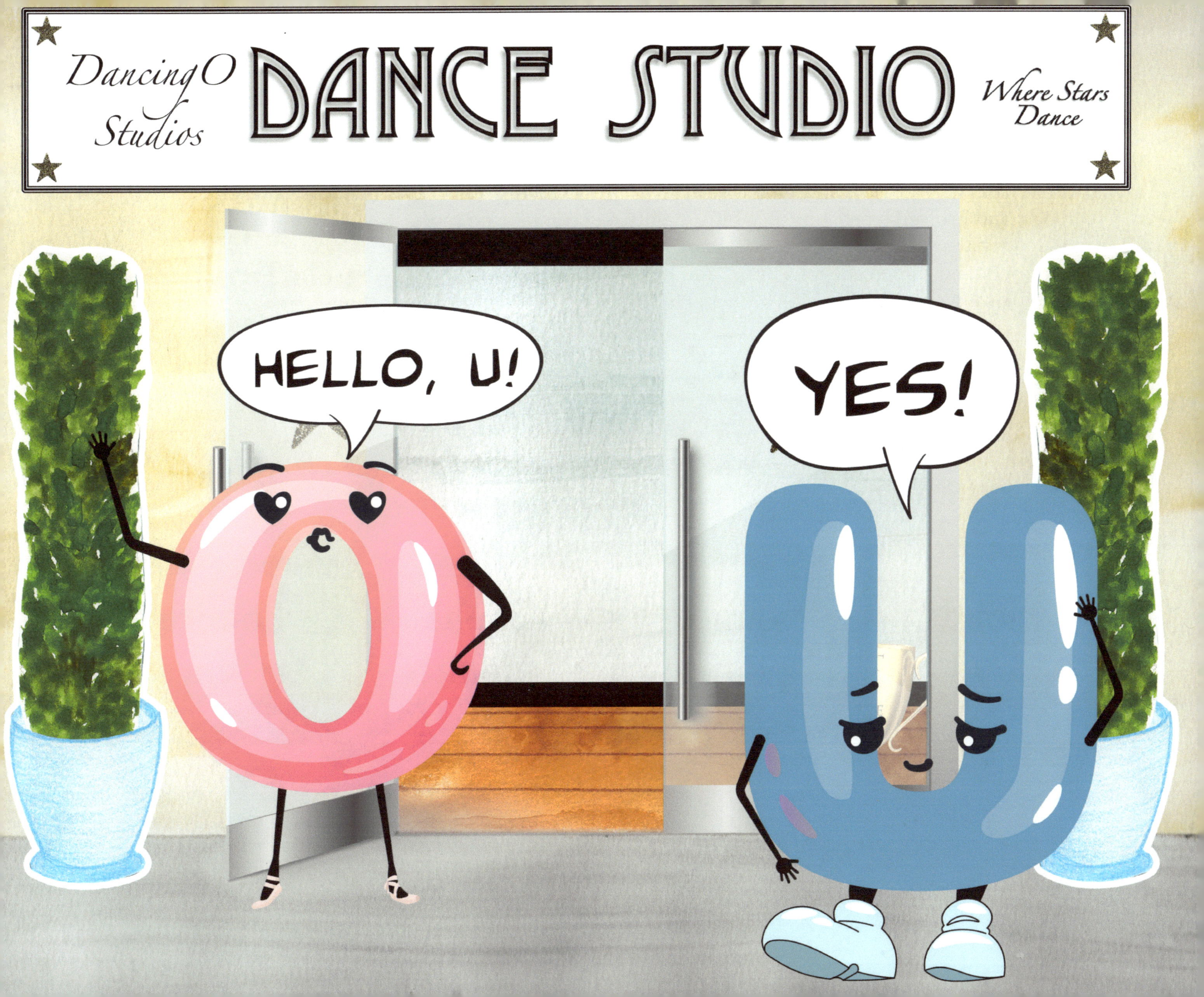

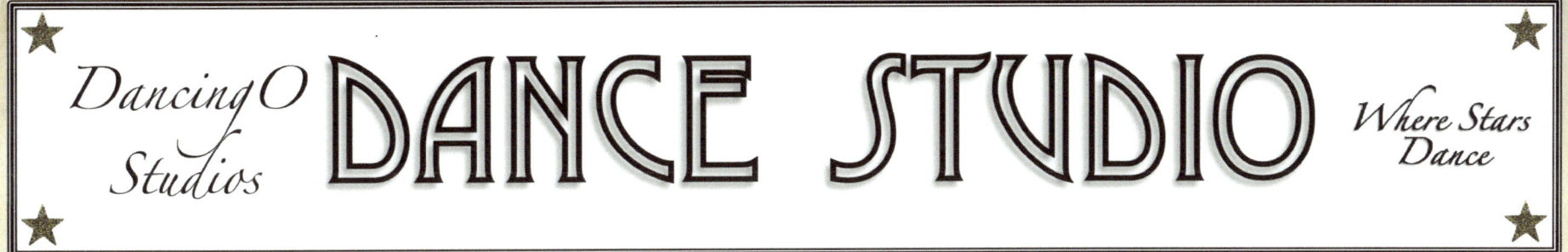

After weeks of preparation, Usual U hears Dancing O crying. He knows her crushed toes, twisted ankles, and bruised teeny-tiny, itty-bitty, dainty feet can take no more.

He understands when she tells him, "You have tried so much and worked so hard, but we both know this will not work." His heart is broken. He will never be Dancing O's partner.

As he leaves the studio with a heavy sigh and tears running down his cheeks, he pines, "I hope I find true love someday."

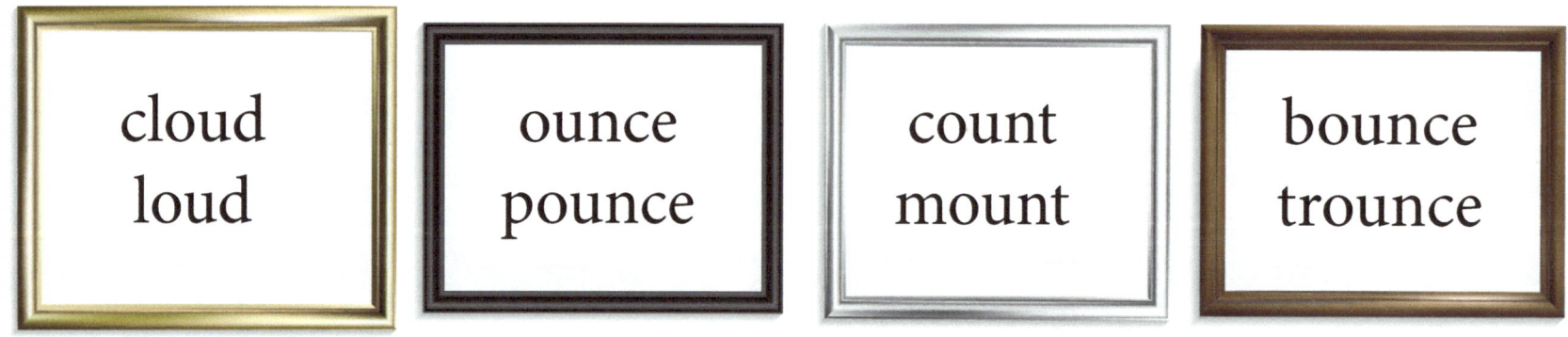

cloud
loud

ounce
pounce

count
mount

bounce
trounce

Gossipy G quickly spreads Usual U's heartbreak story. When Queen Q hears the news, her heart melts. "How could Dancing O not see the sincerity and devotion Usual U offers?" she wonders. "I will invite him for tea to cheer him up."

"A tea party? With me? Oh how lovely." Usual U wears his finest. "Maybe she will not notice my big feet," he hopes.

"Remember to be romantic," encourages lil' sis Lovey V. "Remember to be you," encourages big sis Ms. W.

After many tea parties and much conversation, their friendship grows and blossoms into more. Soon Queen Q realizes that no matter what, her feet will be safe. She only has to tell Usual U.

Queen Q takes the lead, as always, and asks, "Will you be my partner?"

Usual U is unsure, as usual. He begins to worry, as usual. "But my feet. They're so big. I am sorry," he apologizes, as usual.

"No worries. No apologies. See my flare? It protects my feet," continues Queen Q. "So, will you be my partner?"

Usual U smiles. His heart mends. He finds new love with Queen Q. "Yes, of course I'll be your partner!" exclaims Usual U. He can hardly wait to share the news with his sisters! Lovey V—won't she be impressed?! And Ms. W—won't she be thrilled?!

QU are in love and inseparable. Queen Q leads and her feet are safe—just the way she likes it. Usual U follows silently behind the scenes, unnoticed—just the way he likes it.

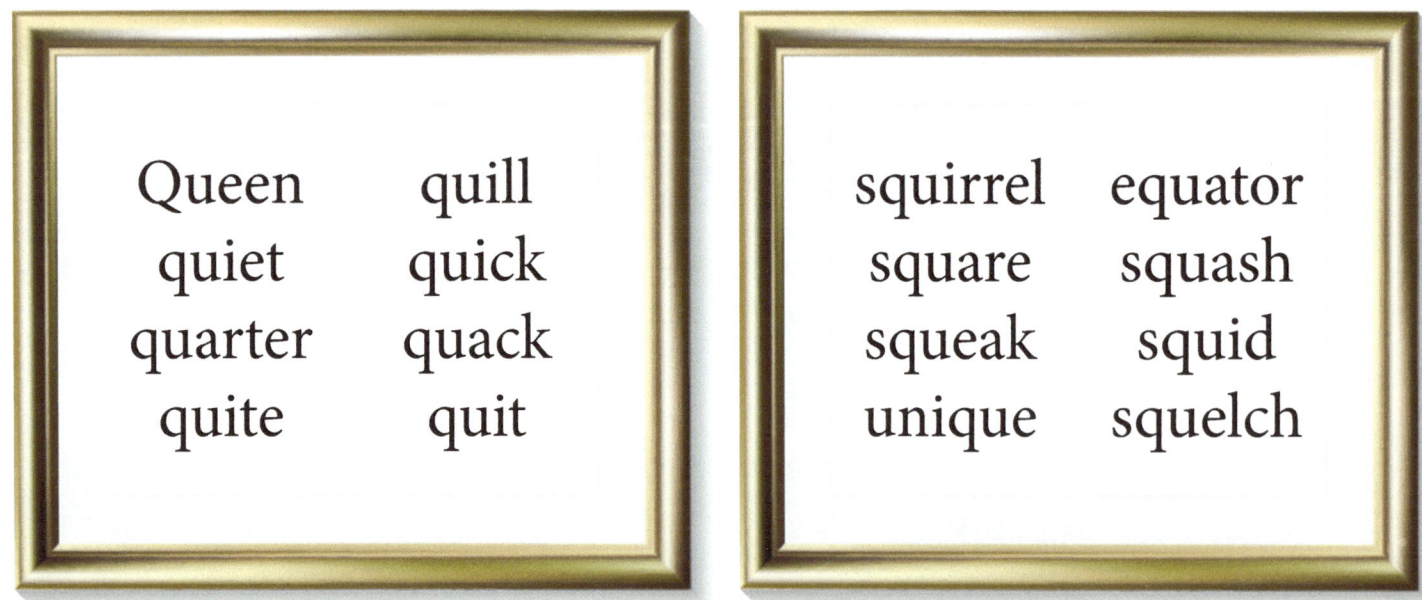

Queen	quill	squirrel	equator
quiet	quick	square	squash
quarter	quack	squeak	squid
quite	quit	unique	squelch

Protective Flair

All the vowels are busy with Dancing O's Walk-n-Talk Dance, all except Usual U. Still feeling the sting of heartbreak from the dance competition, he is fine standing this dance out.

So when Dancing O invites him to her studio, he is stunned as she says, "My itty-bitty, teeny-tiny feet have recovered, and I want to teach you my Walk-n-Talk Dance."

Usual U cannot stop smiling. "How wonderful is this?" he thinks. "Even though we can't be partners, we can be friends."

coupe   soup   troupe

At one of their practices, Usual U knows something is up. Diva A, Sparkling E, and Legend I have been at Dancing O's studio every day for weeks. "But why?" he worries, staring at his big feet.

He arrives at the studio. Everyone is waiting. The music begins. The vowels step into place. Usual U hears Dancing O's voice over the loud speaker. "Announcing! A movie star word. A sparkle word. A legendary word. A word for our friend Usual U. The word? **BEAUTIFUL**.

Usual U is overcome. Happy tears splash on his huge feet. "Thank you, my friends. Thank you, Dancing O. Thank you!" he cries. "Best Walk-n-Talk Dance ever!"

"Group hug," calls Dancing O. "Just watch your toes," they all laugh.

beautiful

Usual U is more worried than usual. The Alphabet Council has decided he is to be a word all on his own. What? That is not how to be unnoticed.

He knows "I" has a word all on his own—but Legend I is, well, a legend. He knows "A" has a word all on her own—but Diva A is, well, a diva. Usual U does not want to be a word all on his own because "U" is, well, usual.

"It's an honor," a proud Queen Q grins. "You can do this," she encourages.

"Not alone. I cannot do this alone. What am I going to do?" asks a very stressed Usual U.

"Let's get help!" suggests Queen Q.

An alphabet all-call for volunteers to help Usual U goes out. Who will answer? Who will join him? Who will silently support him?

Summons

We greet you well

Whereas the second day of June next is appointed for the solemnity of Your Word Coronation.

These are to Will and Command you to make your personal attendance on Us at the time above mentioned furnished and appointed as to your Rank and Quality appertained, there to do a perform all such Services as shall be required belong unto you.

Whereof you are not

And so, We bid you most heartily farewell.

Given at Our Court
this first day of December in
the first year of Our Reign.

By Our Letter Council's Command

Dancing O jumps at the chance to help her friend. "But we will need another letter since together we say 'OUch,'" she reminds the Alphabet Council.

"Can I be in your word?" asks Y-in-Disguise. "I love being disguised in words."

"How great is this?" smiles Usual U.

"First: Y-in-Disguise, hidden."

"Second: Dancing O, quiet."

"Third: ME, saying my name behind the scenes unnoticed. Just the way I like it."

"Then it's decided," announces Queen Q.

The Alphabet Council unanimously approves. Usual U will not have to be his own word.

Grandpa Z happily proclaims, "Three letters spell Usual U's word: YOU. Congratulations. Great teamwork!"

When thinking of Usual U, everyone thinks of, well, usual, because that's what he is: usual. But there is one time when he is not. One time when he is noticed. That one time is in his special word: **UNUSUAL**.

"How come he gets a word with his letter THREE times?" asks his little sis Lovey V. "You know he's just usual."

"He's more than usual. You're just jealous," answers big sis Ms. W.

Grandpa Z explains, "Everyone deserves something special."

"But it is so not me," worries Usual U.

Grandpa Z continues, "Usual U, you have shown you can be so much more than usual. Behind the scenes unnoticed you have handled heartbreak, found true love, conquered your fears, and supported your friends. Your usual is actually unusual."

Blushing, Usual U stammers, "I suppose you are right. Thank you, Grandpa Z."

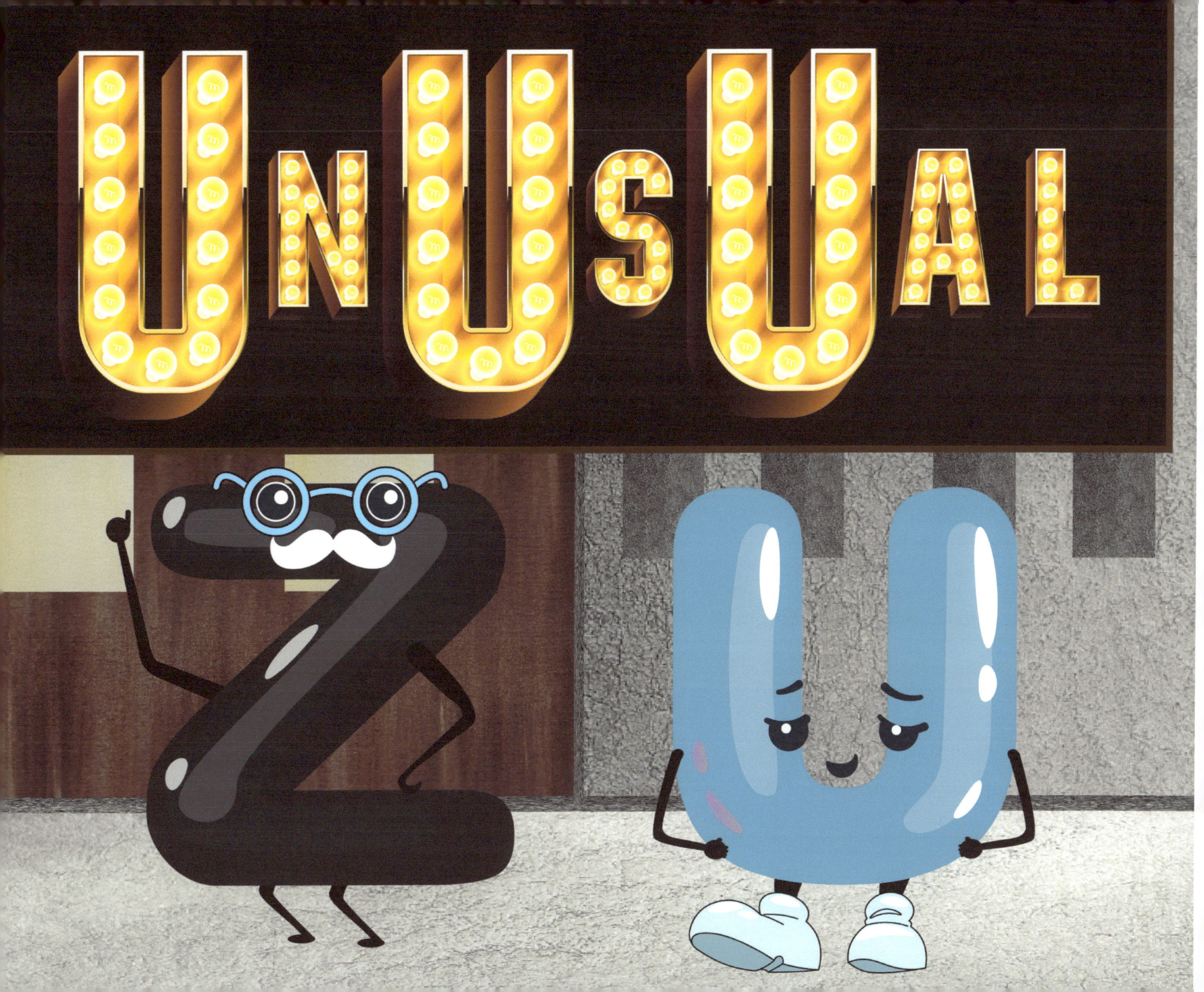
UNUSUAL

Tonight is THE night—the Annual Letter Awards show.

Queen Q adjusts Usual U's bow tie, commenting, "Your shoes from Dancing O's Twinkle Toes look fabulous."

"Do they make my feet look even bigger?" worries Usual U.

"Nope. Besides my feet are safe," replies Queen Q.

As they enter the auditorium, all eyes notice the bow tie, the top hat, the shoes. Wow!

"I am so proud of you," encourages Queen Q. "Better get used to being noticed—at least for tonight."

"This is the best night of my life," smiles Usual U. Then he adds with a twinkle, "Tonight, call me 'Unusual U.' But just for tonight."

What do you do after an awards ceremony?
Crash the after-party!
Everybody from everywhere is here to be seen with everyone!

Queen Q and Unusual U share a lively dance showing off Queen Q's protective flare.
"How quick their feet. How exquisite their outfits," the letters approve.

"How in love," smiles Dancing O.

"How romantic," smiles Lovey V.

"How perfect," smiles Ms. W.

"How impressive," smiles Y-in-Disguise.

Unusual U tips his hat and grins, "I am definitely okay with being noticed tonight!"

About the Author

After receiving her masters in teaching from George Fox University, Theresa Lang thoroughly enjoyed teaching kindergarten and first and second grade for nearly twenty years.

In her classroom, she created a world where the letters can finally talk for themselves and explain the myriad of sounds they produce. Why? Because her students struggled with simple words, often because "one letter makes one sound" does not hold true in English. Her continued passion to help students succeed is the impetus to expose, through her stories, the secret lives of the letters that surround us.

Lang lives in the Pacific Northwest with her cats, Yama and Zuki. She has two grown sons and looks forward to sharing these stories with her grandchildren.

About the Star

After receiving her BA in performance art and design from the University of Letters, Diva A moved to Letterwood to pursue her career in entertainment. She began in print, then moved to TV and movies. The transition to music was simple as her five sounds are so musical.

Before hitting it big in the Biz, Diva A enjoyed designing jeweled crowns as a hobby, which has grown into her Ba-Bling-Bling empire.

Diva A lives in a Letterwood Hills mansion, entertaining often. Her favorite color is gold. She enjoys sushi and traveling the world. Her best friend is Sparkling E. While her manager, Letter I, oversees her affairs, never forget that Diva A is always the boss.

She is most proud of sharing her five sounds since it helps readers decode. She knows once they know her story, they will be encouraged and have confidence to read, plus have fun doing it.

About the Sparkle

After graduating from Letterburg High School having been a student body officer, yearbook editor, volleyball team captain, second chair flute, and baseball statistician; Sparkling E decided to move to Letterwood to be a Diva-in-Training and share her sparkle.

Her endless enthusiasm and energy puts her everywhere, doing everything, and seeing everyone every day. Which explains why her favorite word is: every.

Living in a Letterwood Hills cottage, she is walking distance of her BFF, Diva A. Her favorite color is bubble gum pink. She loves visiting exotic places with *Spoiler Alert* her secret admirer, now partner, X. She always makes time for her twin brother, Legend I. She visits her hometown often to see her mom and dad, M and N.

She is ecstatic to share her story with readers so when they encounter her in a word, they know she is: being a Diva-in-training; or using her sparkling dust—or ran out!; or doing a twin-tastic antic! What she wishes most though is that everyone everywhere knows she is a FRIEND—the sparkliest thing everyone can be.

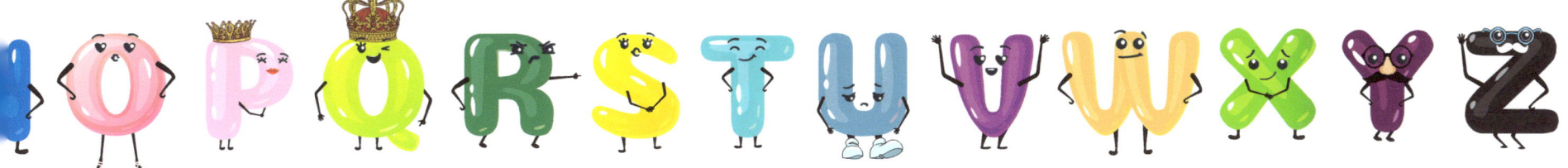

About the Legend

Legend I attended community college where he blossomed in drama club. There he acted, excelled in costume design, and eventually was named director managing the program. Next, he followed his twin sister Sparking E to Letterwood becoming Diva A's manager. Diva A remembered the childhood twin-tastic antics, but she hired him for his organization, creativity, and impeccable fashion style.

He has separate living quarters at Diva A's mansion. His favorite color is rainbow. When his mom and dad (M and N) visit, as his guest, his exclusive permanent capital status gives them unlimited access to all the star-studded events.

He is thrilled to share his story with readers so when they encounter him in a word, they know about his twin-tastic antics with sis E and his work with GH. But the most important thing to remember? He has exclusive permanent capital status to use whenever readers refer to themselves in writing.

About the Dancer

Beginning her dance career at the renowned JLD School of Dance in NYC, Dancing O soon realized she wanted to be where stars dance. She moved to LA to study at the World of Dance Studios. After graduating, she opened her own studio to dance with the vowels (A-E-I-O-U) plus W and Y.

Dancing O lives in a Letterwood high-rise condo with its own dance floor and disco ball. Her favorite color is orange because it begins with O, is a color, and is a fruit. Usual U crushed hard on her, but they make better friends. Her favorite gal-pal is Ms. W.

She has won countless competitions, choreographed for endless dance challenges, and continues to design shoes for her Twinkle Toes shoe shop. Dancing O is most proud of sharing how her Walk-n-Talk Dance helps readers decode vowel sounds. Essentially, she never wants the dancing to stop!

About the Usual

Pursuing his secret crush, Dancing O brought Usual U to Letterwood where he excels at going unnoticed. His uncanny ability to go unnoticed has served him in various occupations. He almost always works behind the scenes. Even his favorite color, gray, goes unnoticed.

He did attain some notoriety when his romance with Dancing O came to an end during their dance competition training. Those big feet of his did quite a number on her tiny feet making for too many "OUches" to endure. But worry not, he found love with Queen Q thanks to her flare. They live in a small farm house and care for their quince orchard. His baby sister Lovely V and older sister Ms. W visit on holidays.

Usual U's favorite job is spelling his word: Y-O-U because he gets to work (behind the scenes) with his two best friends. He is most proud of sharing his story to help readers decode words where he is (regretfully) stepping on O's feet—OUch! Remember, it is okay to be usual because moments to be unusual are always just a footstep away.